Beside
the Sea

THE NEW LUXURY SWIMMING POOL

MORECAMBE AND HEYSHAM

BRITAINS MOST MODERN AND PROGRESSIVE RESORT

EXPRESS SERVICES AND CHEAP TICKETS

WHITLEY BAY

IT'S QUICKER BY RAIL

Cooling our feet

Beside the Sea

Britain's Lost Seaside Heritage

Sarah Freeman

Aurum
Press

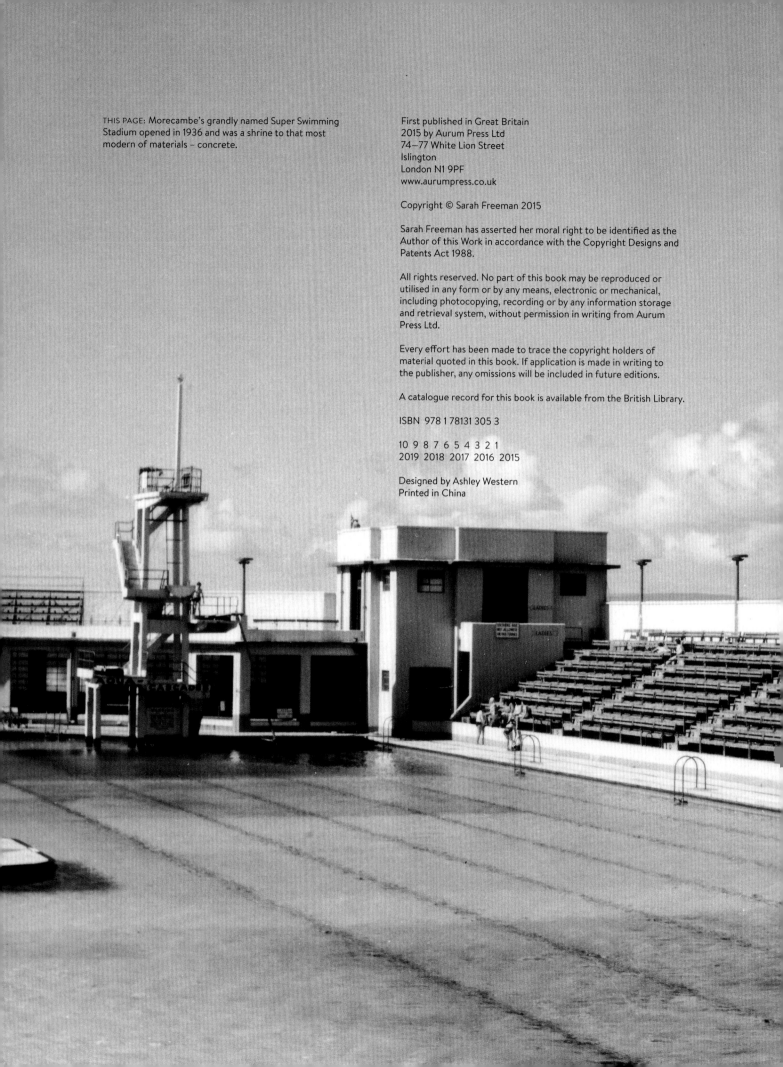

THIS PAGE: Morecambe's grandly named Super Swimming Stadium opened in 1936 and was a shrine to that most modern of materials – concrete.

First published in Great Britain
2015 by Aurum Press Ltd
74—77 White Lion Street
Islington
London N1 9PF
www.aurumpress.co.uk

A catalogue record for this book is available from the British Library.

ISBN 978 1 78131 305 3

10 9 8 7 6 5 4 3 2 1
2019 2018 2017 2016 2015

Designed by Ashley Western
Printed in China

To every stranger who shared a story

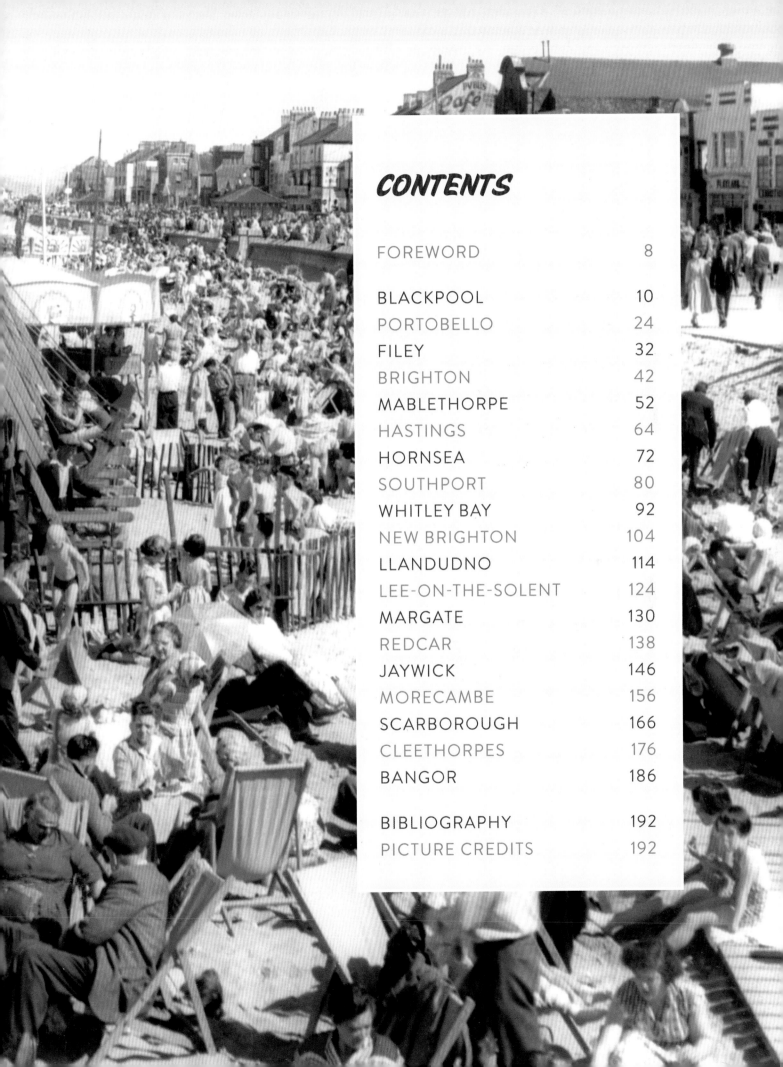

CONTENTS

FOREWORD

There's a famous seaside place called Blackpool
That's made for fresh-air and fun
And Mr and Mrs Ramsbottom went there with young Albert, their son.

THE LION AND ALBERT, MARRIOT EDGAR, 1932

Poets, artists and writers have long been inspired by the coast, but from the 1800s through to the 1960s the British seaside was also where the rest of us found escapism.

It was the Victorians who laid the foundations of the modern seaside resorts and with the arrival of the railways, previously sleepy coastal towns woke up to the opportunities thousands of visitors desperate for entertainment brought.

Grand hotels were built, theatres and dance halls opened their doors and the promenades and piers became a place to see and be seen.

Later the Art Deco age of the 1930s brought hotels with clean lines, lidos and bathing pools and the railway posters, created by some of the most cutting-edge designers of the day, painted idyllic pictures of children clambering on rocks by the water's edge and aspirational couples in the mode of Cary Grant and Doris Day walking along pristine seafronts.

The seaside had glamour and for those who boarded the trains and charabancs from soot-clad industrial cities it also promised the kind of fun captured by artists like Donald McGill on iconic saucy postcards. Those cartoons of buxom landladies and leering men were for a while the symbol of the British seaside. It was a place to let your hair down, a place where anything went and often did.

We became creatures of habit, families going each year, not just to the same guesthouse but to the same spot on the beach and the same table in the nearest pub.

Today, many of the Victorian and Edwardian piers have been reclaimed by the sea, the ballrooms have been turned into bingo halls and the open-air pools filled in with concrete.

In a blink of an eye, seaside glamour turned into the much lampooned wet weekend in Bognor.

Now many of the people's pleasure palaces of yesteryear are blighted by high unemployment and the boarded-up shops are signs that these once thriving resorts are among some of the most deprived areas in the country.

The reasons for the decline are many. In part it was the arrival of cheap foreign holidays, and polluted beaches did little to persuade holidaymakers to stay home, but the truth is the world changed and, for a while, the seaside stood still.

In recent years, preservation trusts have successfully fought to save what's left of Britain's seaside golden age, but for some of those piers, theatres and lidos it was too late. Many had already been claimed by the elements or fallen victim to the architectural mistakes of the 1960s and 1970s, and now the only thing that remains are the memories.

PLEASURE TRIPS
ON

D H DRAGON RAPIDE
SEE THE TOWER
FROM THE AIR
10/-
SQUIRES GATE AIRPORT

FIRST AID

BLACK

POOL

You can always tell when it's Sunday in Blackpool. Late morning, stag and hen parties, weary from the night before, begin to spill out of the seafront guesthouses. Some look hopeful that the sea air will blow away the cobwebs, while others seek sanctuary in one of the bars along the promenade. The front has been given a bit of a lift recently, with £87 million pumped into a regeneration programme, but the makeover has only gone so far. Turn your back to the water and the seafront remains a mix of discount stores, rock shops and amusement arcades.

'That's where it was, right there,' says Barry Shaw of Blackpool's Civic Trust. He's pointing to a modern building, next to the resort's iconic Tower. Slightly obscured by scaffolding, at one end families are having an early lunch at Harry Ramsden's fish and chip shop. At the other, there's Poundland. 'That piece of land was once home to one of the grandest variety theatres this country has ever seen and now look what we've replaced it with. If only we could turn back the clock, I'd like to think we'd do things a little differently.'

The recent history of many of Britain's seaside resorts has often been marred by missed opportunities and the story of Blackpool's Palace Theatre neatly sums up how boom turned to bust.

Wind back to the last few years of the nineteenth century and Blackpool was clear in its ambitions. There were undoubtedly grander seaside resorts, but none was more popular with the masses of the industrial north. Within sixty miles of Blackpool there were eight million factory and mill workers and when the railway arrived in the North West in the 1840s it put them in direct contact.

In the official guidebooks, sponsored by Stone's Original Green Ginger Wine, new safety razors and Borwick's Baking Powder, guesthouses promised the working man's family reasonable lodgings at moderate prices and each page was devoted to some new entertainment they could enjoy. So much was there to do, it was a place, they said, where even the longest day seemed short.

Progress was the town's motto. It appeared on Blackpool's coat of arms and by the mid 1890s that determination to be ahead of the game had already resulted in the building of the 518ft tower and the Winter Gardens. In 1899 it was also the driving force behind the completion of the grandest theatre the town would ever see. The Alhambra, as it was originally known, was not just another venue, it was a work of art.

Built in the Italian Renaissance style, the red-brick and buff terracotta exterior mirrored that of the Tower next door and no detail was left to chance. The

Previous pages: Blackpool targeted working class families from the North of England with colourful advertising which promised fun at an affordable price.

Left: By the end of the nineteenth century the resort already had a reputation for entertainment, with the pier often transformed into a open-air ballroom.

Opposite: The Palace Theatre was ornate both inside and out. When it first opened as the Alhambra in 1899 many likened it to a grand European palace.

THE PALACE BALLROOM, BLACKPOOL.

Within sixty miles of Blackpool there were eight million factory and mill workers and when the railway arrived in the North West in the 1840s it put them in direct contact.

1,494 drawings prepared by architects would have stretched a mile in length and by the time eighteen different firms from London, Liverpool, Leeds and Manchester had completed their sections, labourers had used 3.4 million bricks, 275,500 leaves of gold, 6,500 yards of velvet and 1,500 tonnes of iron. Lavish doesn't even come close.

Home to a theatre, circus and ballroom, the men behind the scheme could hardly wait to show the Alhambra off and on 4 July 1899, journalists from all over the country were invited to take a tour in the hope that when they returned to their desks they would have nothing but praise for a town taking the business of entertainment so seriously.

Filing neatly through the circus where an acrobat, bowing to the empty benches, was practising for opening night, they tested the parquet-sprung floor in the ballroom and marvelled at how every seat in the theatre had a good view of the stage. One was overheard to say that it looked less like a theatre and more like a grand European palace. He was right. No expense had been spared. Those floors not laid with marble were instead covered with thick crimson carpet, in the restaurant the walls had been lined with Venetian mosaics and anyone looking up at the ceiling in the ballroom would have seen the handiwork of mastercraftsman J.M. Boekbinder. Borrowing from the Greek myths, the central panel showed Apollo arriving triumphant from Olympus to bestow music and arts upon the world.

'Much has been written of the magnificence of ancient Rome and the cities of Italy,' began the official guide to the Alhambra's construction. 'But we are quite certain that when Julius Caesar and his friends used to shake the dust of the Forum off their feet and run down to Pompeii from a Saturday to Monday, that pleasure resort could not boast an arena whose halls and vestibules showed such a galaxy of marbles as the Alhambra presents.'

That may well have been the first and last time anyone noticed a similarity between Blackpool's

Left: The Victorian age was all about grand architectural statements, none more extravagant than Blackpool's lavishly decorated Tower Ballroom.

seafront and Roman antiquity, but the Alhambra was undeniably beautiful. With its electric lighting and state-of-the-art lift it was also seen as a sign of faith in Blackpool's future. However, as the very first visitors queued up at the entrance kiosk it quickly became clear to those responsible for balancing the books that there was a serious problem. The circus could hold 2,000 and the theatre and the ballroom could accommodate 3,000 each. However, in order to compete with Blackpool's other attractions they couldn't exceed the standard sixpenny entrance fee. Even if all three venues were packed each night, the Alhambra would still never cover its costs.

So as young couples danced afternoons away in the ballroom and as the balconies overlooking the front filled with those content just to take the sea air, behind the scenes the money men were becoming increasingly anxious. Just three years after that grand opening, the Alhambra was forced into liquidation and when it failed to sell at auction it looked like it might be one of Blackpool's most expensive ever mistakes.

However, when a few months later the savvy lot at the Tower Company snapped it up for a knock-down £140,000, it paved the way for a new era. Going back to basics, the circus was turned into a cinema and rebranded as the Palace, the new theatre

'The audiences were always wonderful, you could feel that they wanted to have a good time. Their applause was our reward for what could be a very lonely life.'

management had just one thing in their sights – music hall. They knew that those arriving into Blackpool Central Station, which spewed visitors directly out on to the Golden Mile packed with fortune-tellers, tarot card readers, phrenologists and card sharks, wanted to be entertained. They wanted song and dance acts, they wanted close-up magic, jugglers and comedians. They wanted artists like the Scottish singer and entertainer Harry Lauder and the male impersonator Vesta Tilley, and the Palace's master of ceremonies, Lal Wright, was happy to provide. In a previous life, Lal had been Blackpool Football Club's first ever goalkeeper, but the stage was his natural home. As well as his own act – featuring an elephant on roller skates – Lal was also the perfect host, encouraging those taking their first faltering steps into show business and keeping a tight rein on some of the bigger stars who would occasionally arrive at his door, tape measure in hand, demanding to know why their name wasn't in bigger letters on the bills outside.

These acts didn't come cheap. Tilley, whom one critic said sang so beautifully the 'audience's tears were in danger of washing the theatre away', commanded up to £300 a week, while Lauder refused to get out of bed for anything less than £500. Yet without them, the Palace knew its audience would simply go elsewhere. Most were booked months in advance, but every Monday morning any last-minute gaps on the bill would be plugged by acts on that week's agents lists. It made for an eclectic mix. By the 1930s, the Palace had established itself as the region's number one variety theatre and its headline acts read like a who's who of British entertainment royalty.

It was the Palace where George Formby made his Blackpool debut, it was where Tony Hancock, Norman Wisdom and Benny Hill all honed their comic timing and it was where the audience got to hear Vera Lynn sing 'We'll Meet Again' and 'The White Cliffs of Dover'.

'It was one of those theatres every star wanted to perform at,' says Dame Vera, who made her first public performance at the age of seven. A regular at the Palace, in 1951 she was in Blackpool for the full fifteen-week summer season. 'The audiences were always wonderful, you could feel that they wanted to have a good time. Their applause was our reward for what could be a very lonely life. After the matinee performance most of the acts would go back to their boarding house for a rest to ensure they were on top form for the two evening shows. I know people think that we must have had a wonderful time, all socialising together, but it really wasn't like that at all.'

There were others acts now forgotten and swallowed up by the mists of time. Performers like Sticky Simon the Human Flypaper and the Polish-

Opposite: Dame Vera Lynn trod the boards at Blackpool many times in the 1950s and 1960s. She returned in 1983 and was photographed here with Second World War veterans.

Right: Holidaymakers often bumped into famous faces in between performances. Here, in 1953, Morecambe and Wise took time out on the sands.

Far right: The Palace Theatre was also where entertainer George Formby, who turned ukulele playing into an art form, first performed for Blackpool audiences.

born magician Horace Goldin, who in 1915 made a Bengal tiger disappear on the Palace stage and who returned a few years later to do the same to his glamorous assistant and a grand piano. Then there was Chung Ling Soo, who caught bullets on a dinner plate at the Palace in 1917 and who attracted more attention in death than he ever did alive. A few months after his Blackpool appearance, Soo, who was in fact plain old William Ellsworth Robinson, died on stage at London's Wood Green Empire when his trick went tragically wrong.

In the foreword to the 1924 official guide to Blackpool, Harold Whiteside wrote: 'After you have once tasted a Blackpool holiday, all other holidays are like weak tea beside champagne.'

Most of those who packed into the guesthouses had never drunk so much as a glass of champagne, but they knew what they liked and it tasted like Blackpool. The outbreak of the Second World War effectively mothballed many resorts, but even that couldn't dent its fortunes.

Box office takings remained steady thanks to the presence of thousands of RAF personnel who had been sent to the town for basic training, and

the promotional brochures published ahead of the 1940 summer season were almost a call to arms: 'In the best of times and in times when you need it most, Blackpool attracts a welcome relief,' went the introduction. 'You owe it to yourself to have a really good holiday this year and it is Blackpool's duty and pleasure to give it to you.'

However, while the Palace had survived both financial mismanagement and the war, there was one thing it couldn't compete with: Television. While at the beginning of the 1950s few families owned their own set, by the end of the decade the nation's appetites had been whetted and, compared to the new breed of stars who appeared nightly in living rooms, music hall began to look a little old-fashioned. The beginning of the end for the Palace came in 1957 when it announced that for the first time in its history it would shut during the winter months. Most knew then that the writing was on the wall, although the summer season limped on for a few more years.

It was much the same atmosphere on the Golden Mile where no one paid much attention to the young man, hoarse from shouting into a microphone about

Left: As the years went by families seeking thrills and spills began spending more time – and money – at the Pleasure Beach than they were in the Palace Theatre.

Opposite: In Blackpool's heyday it was often difficult to see the sand between the deckchairs, but the resort's iconic Tower was always visible.

'You owe it to yourself to have a really good holiday this year and it is Blackpool's duty and pleasure to give it to you.'

some new freak show exhibit nobody wanted to see. 'It had all become a bit seedy,' says Barry Shaw. 'There was a gradual realisation that Blackpool, once always ahead of the game, had become stuck in the past.'

Confirmation of the closure of the Palace came in the *Blackpool Evening Gazette* on 7 March 1961. However, the few paragraphs on the front page were overshadowed by news that a package of drugs had been flown in from the US for Elizabeth Taylor who was being treated for respiratory problems in a London clinic.

The report inside seemed equally unconcerned about the Palace's future. The building would be knocked down following that year's summer season starring Frankie Vaughan and from the rubble would rise a new Lewis's department store. It would be the biggest redevelopment in Blackpool since the war and would signal a new, modern chapter for the resort.

Two days later, when thousands gathered for the funeral of George Formby a few miles down the road in Liverpool, they might have been mourning the passing of all musical hall variety acts. The world had moved on.

There was no outcry on the letters pages of the *Gazette* to the Palace proposals, where more ire was directed towards British Rail's policy of charging for dogs than those planning to demolish a slice of Blackpool history.

'At the time no one thought much about heritage,' says Barry Band, who a decade later would be involved in the successful campaign to save Blackpool's Grand Theatre. 'There were just two types of buildings: old ones and new ones. When places became a bit tatty, you knocked them down and started again. That was just how it was.

Right: The origins of Blackpool's world famous illuminations date back to the 1870s when a series of lights was installed along the promenade.

'However, there was another problem with the Palace. The way it had been designed made it almost impossible to adapt. The only way would have been to rip out the interior and if all you had been left with was the façade it would have defeated the object a little.

'The truth was the Palace was too big to make money. It always had been. In show business people forget that without the business there ain't no show. Ultimately that's what did for the Palace.'

The final concert saw Vaughan joined on stage by Hetty King, who had performed at the opening night of the Alhambra in 1899. King was one of a number of popular impersonators who had donned top hats, tails and facial hair to satirise male behaviour. Originating in America, the acts had been embraced by British audiences, but seemed out of place by the 1960s, a decade which would belong to the feminist movement.

'I remember when the big cranes went up with the wrecking balls,' says Barry Shaw, his collar turned up against the biting wind. 'No one really took much notice. I suppose it seemed like the right thing for Blackpool at the time. There was a feeling maybe that we were in danger of being left behind.'

Some of the Palace's many thousands of bricks ended up being used in the construction of the M60 motorway. Lewis's closed down in the early 1990s and in the intervening years a number of businesses have come and gone.

However, just opposite where the theatre once stood there is a lasting tribute to the town's music-hall heyday. Blackpool's Comedy Carpet was designed by artist Gordon Young as a reminder that the town had once been a 'magnetic chuckle point for the nation'. It features the jokes, catchphrases and songs of 1,000 comedians. Most are long gone, but on this stretch of the promenade they still manage to raise a smile.

Left: The Comedy Carpet, a tribute to entertainers past and present, is believed to be Britain's largest piece of public art.

PORTO

BELLO

Amid the hundreds of thousands of entries in the *Oxford English Dictionary*, a few lines are devoted to a Great British seaside institution.

Ninety-nine Brit. (also 99), an ice cream cone made with soft ice cream with a stick of flaky chocolate inserted into it. [Apparently an arbitrary marketing name. The original ice cream contained Cadbury's '99' Flake (produced specially for the ice cream trade) but the application to the chocolate may not precede its application to the ice cream.]

An arbitrary marketing name? Not according to the Arcari family. They also dispute claims by Cadbury's that it was one of their sales managers in County Durham who coined the phrase sometime in the early 1930s. The Arcaris say they were selling 99s a full ten years before its first appearance in Cadbury's price list in 1935. In fact, they insist the ice cream cone with a chocolate flake was named after their ice cream parlour, which just so happened to be at 99 Portobello High Street.

The business was started by Stephen Arcari, who came to Scotland from Italy following the First World War, and it was he, according to his granddaughter Mandy, who first broke a Flake in half and pressed it into a scoop of vanilla ice cream.

'People liked it and so he kept selling it. We're not sure of the exact date, but it was not long after he opened the shop in 1922. We think that one of the Cadbury's reps might have come to Portobello, seen Granddad selling 99s and taken the idea back to the company's headquarters. We have challenged the *Oxford English Dictionary*, but the problem is there is no written evidence, nothing on paper, so while we all know how the 99 came about, we can't prove it.'

When Stephen died aged just fifty, the ice-cream business passed to his son, Rudy. A familiar figure around the seaside town just three miles from Edinburgh in his blue overalls and ever-burning cigar, it was he who turned Arcari's Ice Creams into a Portobello institution.

'Everyone knew Dad and growing up, friends used to think we were so lucky to have an ice cream parlour – they used to think we had knickerbocker glories for breakfast, dinner and tea.

'Throughout the 1970s and 1980s, as well as the shop we had around sixteen vans going around this part of Edinburgh during the summer, all supplied with ice cream from a factory Dad had set up. Everyone knew the name Arcari and that was really down to him. He put his heart and soul into the business.'

The much-loved ice cream parlour is now a hairdresser's. However, long before it closed in 2005, Portobello had already lost some of its most iconic attractions.

Over the years the resort has been home to Scotland's first and last pleasure pier, an impressive

EDINBURGH MARINE GARDENS PORTOBELLO

Previous pages: Portobello's open-air swimming pool, which opened in 1936, was where a young Sean Connery worked as a lifeguard.

Left: Edinburgh Marine Gardens were moved building by building from the other side of the city, reopening in Portobello in 1909.

Right: The family of Italian Stephen Arcari believe he invented the iconic 99 ice cream despite a counterclaim from Cadbury's.

Somali Village, Edinburgh Marine Gardens,
Portobello, 1910
GROUP OF WOMEN AND CHILDREN

Left: The gardens included a recreation of a traditional Somali settlement, complete with mud huts and 70 native Africans.

Below: Portobello pier opened in 1871, but its history was short. Repeated storm damage took its toll and it was finally demolished in 1917.

lido, boasting the country's first wave machine, and for a while its attractions also included a human zoo.

Edinburgh Marine Gardens was the kind of ambitious and slightly bonkers project that characterised the Victorian age. On 1 May 1908, Prince Arthur of Connaught officially opened the Scottish National Exhibition in the capital's Saughton Park. The previous winter, a small army of labourers had built a series of white stucco buildings to create a brand new village for an event designed to last just six months. The Palace of Industries housed a showcase of Dutch, Italian and Canadian industry and culture, while outside there was a programme of historical pageants and military tournaments. For those not interested in demonstrations on the use of ammonia sulphate in manure or the displays of Highland weaponry, there was an amusement park, complete with water chute. The exhibition was a major success, attracting more than 3.5 million visitors, which is why when it closed that December a group of businessmen had the idea of moving it, white stucco buildings and all, to Portobello. The concert hall, fine art buildings and Winter Garden tearooms were all carefully dismantled, loaded on to trucks and then rebuilt on a 30-acre site just a twenty-minute drive down the road.

The Pier, Portobello   Valentine's Series

PORTOBELLO OPEN AIR BATHING POOL.
Total Cost (approx.) £90,000.
Length 330 ft.   Width 150 ft.   Area 1·13 acres.   Five Diving Stages from 12 ft. to 32 ft. 8 ins. high.
Accommodation for 6000 Spectators.   Lockers for 1284 Bathers.   Artificial Wave up to 3 ft. high can be developed.

DOWN THE CHUTE, PORTOBELLO SWIMMING POOL

Left: The opening of Portobello's outdoor swimming pool was a major coup for the resort, which needed a flagship attraction to boost visitor numbers.

Right: One of the pool's main draws was its state-of-the-art wave machine, which could create waves more than 3ft high.

Below right: On summer days there were often long queues to get into the pool, which was heated by the power station next door.

Its Art Deco design stood in sharp contrast to the nearby red-brick power station opened by King George V a decade earlier.

'At the time labour was cheap and there was a lot of it around,' says local historian Margaret Munro. 'But it was still an incredible feat to have the site open by the following May. There was nothing the Marine Gardens didn't have. There was a grand ballroom, roller-skating rink, zoo and a scenic railway. When the people of Portobello woke up and discovered they had all this on their doorstep, it must have been a very exciting day.'

One of the more peculiar attractions was the Somali village. Seventy native Somalis had been shipped over from Africa to live in mud huts and to be gawped at by members of the public. These human zoos, or ethnological expositions as they were called

by those who staged them, had taken off across Europe from the 1870s. They were billed as a serious exposition of foreign cultures, but as they staged mock battles and carried out their tribal rituals most of the visitors just pointed and laughed at what they saw as their strange and slightly barbaric ways.

While Portobello's newly-acquired African population no doubt struggled through that year's typical Scottish winter, the businessman who had funded the Gardens to the tune of £25,000 fared, initially at least, rather better. In the first twelve months of opening, 750,000 people paid the seven pence entrance fee and even when one of the young animal trainers was mauled by two panthers backstage

at Bostock's Circus it didn't deter the crowds. In fact, a report about the incident in the local paper admitted the sight of the blood-soaked woman as she was carried away for treatment caused nothing more than 'an unpleasant sensation' among the audience who had been waiting for the next performance.

'I don't think there's any doubt that Edinburgh Marine Gardens were a success, but they were never the same after the First World War,' says Margaret. 'When the site was taken over by the military, troops were billeted in a number of buildings. It did partially reopen, but when the military returned during the Second World War that really was it. When you look at the old postcards of the place it's impossible not to be nostalgic and wish it had survived. There are car showrooms on the site now and it takes quite a lot of imagination to think it was once home to a quite magical pleasure park.'

Edinburgh Marine Gardens had just six years of full use, but by the time they closed and the buildings were dismantled for a second and final time, another Portobello landmark had also been demolished. The opening of the 1,250ft pier on 23 May 1871 had been a big day for the resort. Many seaside towns south of the border already boasted pleasure piers and some saw its completion as crucial to continued economic success. The pier had been designed by leading Scottish railway engineer Sir Thomas Bouch. A few years later he would be castigated following the collapse of another of his projects – the Tay Rail Bridge – just eighteen months after it opened, but for now he was the toast of Portobello. Special

trains were laid on and that afternoon thousands walked along the wooden decking, stopping for refreshments at the pierhead café and queuing for the camera obscura.

With a newly-formed regatta club holding a series of competitions and Firth of Forth paddle steamers now able to stop off at Portobello, the pier made the town busier than ever before. However, come the winter, when the holidaymakers had gone, the iron structure was left to the bitter elements. As repair bills escalated, the pier began to rot. By 1917, it was no longer financially viable and its demolition began. The loss of the pier was hard to bear for those involved in Portobello's tourist industry. Throughout the following

Left: The fortunes of the open-air
pool changed quickly. Closed in
the late 1970s, it soon fell into a
state of disrepair.

Below: Rudy Arcari was a familiar
figure in Portobello, running both
an ice cream parlour and a fleet
of vans.

three decades various proposals for a replacement were put forward, but none ever made it off the drawing board. However, everyone agreed that the resort needed a major new attraction and in 1936 it got one – a brand new open-air swimming pool.

Its Art Deco design stood in sharp contrast to the nearby red-brick power station opened by King George V a decade earlier. Not that anyone seemed to mind, perhaps because, as well as supplying the electricity requirements of Edinburgh's rapidly expanding population, it would also heat the swimming pool.

'Well, they said it was heated by the power station, not that you'd have known,' says Margaret. 'I remember the water being pretty freezing, but it didn't matter. It used to take two buses to get to Portobello from where I lived as a child. It was a big day out and the swimming pool was where you spent most of your time. The waves would reach more than 3ft high and just before the machine was switched on there was a Tannoy announcement advising people who were not strong swimmers to get out of the water – it was so loud that the people in the tenements next door could hear it.'

The open-air pool was where a young Sean Connery worked as a lifeguard before James Bond came calling and it informed the childhood memories of a thousand youngsters like Margaret. During the 1950s and 1960s the terraces were packed and on the busiest summer days, as the queue stretched down the road, it was a case of one in, one out. However, the fortunes of seaside resorts can change as quickly as the tide and a decade later the once lengthy queues had been replaced by a trickle of bathers willing to brave the icy waters. When the power station closed in 1977 most reckoned the pool would be next. And so it came to

pass. The doors were shut the following year.

'It wasn't actually demolished for almost another ten years,' says Margaret. 'The pool closed because not enough people used it, but I think there is a lot of regret that it was allowed to go. It was a beautiful building and a lot of the lidos that did survive are now thriving again.'

Today there are football pitches where the open-air pool once was. They are better used than the lido was in its later years, but when they featured in the opening scenes of *Trainspotting*, Danny Boyle's film about drug addiction and poverty in genteel Edinburgh, it wasn't exactly the kind of publicity Portobello needed.

As tourism declined, Rudy Arcari scaled back his fleet of ice cream vans and the theme tune 'Lara's Theme', from the film *Dr Zhivago*, was heard a little less around the town. The family still make ice cream in a nearby factory, but the news of Rudy's death in May 2014 reminded many of the summers they had spent on Portobello beach.

'It was overwhelming really,' says Mandy. 'Dad had sold ice creams to three generations of some families round here. He'd been diagnosed with stomach cancer in January, but he was still putting in fourteen-hour shifts until a few weeks before he died. We asked him if he wanted to stop working, but he just turned to us and said, "Why would I want to do that? This is my life".'

F I L

E   Y

The Bay in Filey is pretty typical of modern holiday developments. Beside the cottages lining Sunrise Drive, there's a putting course, an indoor swimming pool as well as a sauna and steam room. If you can't be bothered to cook, there's also an Italian coffee shop and a pub claiming to do the best Sunday roasts on the coast.

Had he still been with us, Billy Butlin would no doubt have approved. The Bay is built on the site of one of his very first holiday camps and, while it might be more understated than those first developments, Billy knew two things – to survive in the leisure industry you have to give guests what they want and you can't be afraid of change.

By the time he arrived on the Yorkshire coast in the late 1930s, the South African-born entrepreneur had already opened two camps in Clacton and Skegness, but Filey was to become the jewel in the crown of his empire. Construction was already well underway when war broke out, and with the site requisition by the RAF it wasn't until the final weeks of the 1945 season that the first holidaymakers started to file through the gates. Still clutching their ration books, they were desperate to escape the postwar gloom and Billy was happy to oblige.

Jim Brown was typical of those early guests. In 1947, he had just returned home to Hull from the Far East where he had been serving with the Royal Corps of Signals. Keen to meet up with friends, and by way of celebration, they booked a week at the East Coast's brand new attraction.

'Funnily enough the accommodation and canteen weren't too dissimilar to what we'd had in the army, so we felt quite at home,' says Jim, now in his eighties.

Their military training also came in useful in making the most of the camp's basic amenities. 'We'd been split into two chalets at either end of a long row of accommodation. However, we soon realised that the central heating pipe ran the full length of the chalets. Two of us had been wireless operators, so we used to tap out messages in Morse code. It was nothing top secret, more like, "We'll be ready in ten minutes" or "See you in the bar". Another of our party was a trained electrician and wherever he went he always carried a screwdriver. It came in useful that week as after being rudely awakened by a recording of "Zip-a-dee-doo-dah, My oh my what a wonderful day" on the first morning he swiftly dismantled the Tannoy system.'

Over the years, a number of Filey's loudspeakers would suffer the same fate, but for most the relentlessly cheery daily announcement that 'Rain, hail, wind or shine, it's always a wonderful day at Butlin's' was nothing more than a minor irritant.

On arrival, each guest was given an enamel badge. It suggested membership of an exclusive club and

Previous pages: Charlie the Elephant, pictured here in 1959, was one of Filey's most famous residents, but his move from the Ayr camp didn't go entirely smoothly.

Left: The accommodation at Butlin's was basic, but most holidaymakers didn't spend long in their chalets.

Billy knew two things – to survive in the leisure industry you have to give guests what they want and you can't be afraid of change.

Above: Butlin's had its own train station at Filey. In its heyday, thousands would pour onto the platform each week to be greeted by the camp's Redcoats.

Right: When they checked in, guests were given an enamel badge. Should they ever leave the site, they had to show it to be readmitted.

Far right: Billy Butlin helped transform Britain's tourism industry with his promise of 'a week's holiday for a week's wages'.

This page: The Butlin's philosophy was to take the stress out of family holidays with a full programme of entertainment for both adults and children alike.

assured that they would be readmitted should they leave the camp. Most, however, didn't stray far. There was no need. This mini-town had everything. You might have had to pay a little extra for a private bathroom, and in those early years the biggest luxury the chalets had to offer was a free sample of Velvet tissues, but no one came to Butlin's for a comfortable mattress.

At its height, the Filey camp attracted 10,000 visitors a week, plus a few extra youngsters from nearby Primrose Valley who would sneak through a gap deliberately cut in the fence.

Tony Peers was the compère at Filey in 1973. He didn't come from a family of entertainers – his father drove a petrol tanker and his grandfather had been a miner. In fact, he'd never even been on holiday, but as with many of the Redcoats, show business seemed a decent alternative to a lifetime on a factory production line or hauling coal.

'I was always the class clown and becoming a Redcoat was a way of making a career out of comedy,' says Tony, who ended up settling just down the coast from Filey, in Scarborough, where he still runs one of the country's five remaining summer shows. 'The accommodation was basic, but life was pretty basic back then and we didn't have high expectations.

'The wardrobe had curtains rather than doors; instead of a fitted carpet there was a rug and the food wasn't exactly gourmet although there was plenty of it. After the evening meal they would serve cheese and biscuits. I'd often open my act later that night and ask the women how many of them had a serviette, two cream crackers and a triangle of cheese in their handbags. Hundreds of arms would shoot up. They'd got wise. They knew once dinner had gone there would be no chance of food before breakfast.

'Britain in the 1950s and 1960s was a pretty grey world. Most people rarely ventured more than a mile from their home. They walked to work and on a weekend they went to the local pub. Butlin's offered something different. It even had themed pubs before any of the big breweries caught on to the idea.'

Life at Butlin's was an endless round of knobbly knees' competitions, pageants for holiday princesses and glamorous grannies, swimming galas and whist drives.

No expense was spared at Filey. The Beachcomber Bar, modelled on a Hawaiian theme, had a stream running through it and a volcano which erupted on the hour. Then there was the Crazy Horse Saloon, packed with Wild West paraphernalia, and the oak-panelled Parliament Bar, a replica of the one in the House of Commons. When Billy had an idea, no matter how outlandish, he expected it to be delivered.

In 1957 he decided that he wanted to move an elephant called Charlie from the Ayr camp to Filey. Charlie had first made headlines when a travelling circus, unable to find a trailer robust enough to transport him from one site to another, put him up for sale. Billy had stepped in, but now he faced the same problem. Charlie was 11ft high, 18ft long, not far shy of 8 tonnes and at twenty-four years old he was still growing. The team at Ayr had managed to persuade Charlie on to a low-level trailer, but when he took out a number of telegraph poles and a couple of shop awnings the operation had to be aborted. Not to be defeated, Billy turned to the press, offering £1,000 to anyone willing to move the elephant, described as the largest in captivity.

One bright spark suggested suspending Charlie between two helicopters, Oxford University's department of engineering put forward a solution involving barrage balloons, while a hypnotist offered to lead the elephant down the 300 miles from Scotland in a trance. Just as Billy was beginning to despair, zoologist Andrew Wilson walked into his office, with designs for a special steel crate under his arm. Wilson, who worked with the renowned elephant expert Colonel J.H. Williams, never said how much the move cost, except that it was significantly more than £1,000. It didn't matter. Billy had wanted Charlie moved and, as with most things, he eventually got his way.

'Billy Butlin was a man who made things happen,' says Tony. 'The Filey camp was the Las Vegas of its day. It allowed ordinary families to meet Mr Saturday Night TV and for those of us who worked there it was the first rung on the ladder of show business.'

Along with their uniform every new Redcoat was issued with a rulebook, a bible on behaviour in the camp. 'Mix and mingle,' the guide began. 'Do not spend all your time with one particular family or crowd of campers, no matter how friendly you become. There are others just as deserving of your attention. Do not seek out the young and attractive, they will have no trouble making friends. Look for elderly campers, families and those on their own.'

Redcoats were also told the maximum time they could spend in the bar was fifteen minutes, lateness would not be tolerated and anyone at a loose end during mealtimes must 'swan' the dining room talking to as many guests as possible. It's not quite how Malcolm Deighton remembers it. In the early 1960s he spent the winters working in Hull as a butcher. Come the summer he was Jackie Vernon, a Filey Redcoat entertaining holidaymakers in the 3,000-seat Gaiety Theatre, which was one of the largest venues in Europe when it opened in 1960.

'One of my standing gags was, "One of the guys from security came knocking on the chalet door the other night. He wanted to know whether I'd got a woman in there with me. When I said no, he opened the door and threw one in".'

For most Redcoats, the most important rule *not* in the guide book was 'Don't get caught.'

Billy had thought of everything. For those holidaying on their own there was the One Alone singles club; families with young children could sign up for the services of the chalet patrol nurse, allowing them to enjoy the evening's entertainment safe in the knowledge that someone was keeping an eye (or at the very least an ear) on their little ones. From that first early morning call to the final rousing rendition of 'Goodnight Campers', sung to the melody of

Opposite: Along with its glamorous granny and bathing beauties competitions, Butlin's was perhaps best known for promoting Britain's knobbly knees.

'Goodnight, Sweetheart' each night in the ballroom, life at Butlin's was an endless round of knobbly knees competitions, pageants for holiday princesses and glamorous grannies, swimming galas and whist drives.

'At breakfast I'd get up on stage and read out the events for the next day,' says Malcolm. 'It probably sounds a little regimented, but it never struck us as odd back then. Every Redcoat was given different events to oversee and on an evening I'd be back in the food hall spinning what looked like a giant roulette wheel. The winning table would get a bottle of something fizzy and I remember one evening when I walked over to pop the cork and it came out with so much force that it hit the ceiling and came back down in one man's dessert. He was covered in peaches and cream. I was mortified, although the rest of the campers were in hysterics. Butlin's was a place people came to escape and it was the same for the Redcoats. We worked sixteen hours a day and the pay wasn't great, but you felt like you were part of something much bigger.'

Students who found work at Butlin's during the summer holidays could often be found lying flat out on the thin stretch of grass between the staff chalets after working a sixty-hour week scrubbing floors and washing pots, but most of the holidaymakers didn't notice. They were too busy heading for the boating lake, the miniature railway and the chairlifts.

Billy's formula of a week's holiday for a week's wage where everything you needed was onsite was one that served the camps well as Britain emerged blinking into the postwar years and the family did its best to adapt to changing times.

The early morning Tannoy call was phased out in the mid-1970s, the word 'camp', by then deemed too down-market, was changed to 'holiday centre', and the 'Lads' and 'Lasses' signs on every single toilet were replaced by 'Ladies' and 'Gentlemen'. Even the Redcoats relaxed a little and were no longer insistent on everyone joining in. However, the attempts at modernisation weren't enough to save Filey. Confirmation came in October 1983. By then Sir Billy, who had been knighted in 1964, had been dead three years and it was left to his adopted son Bobby to announce that both Filey and Clacton camps were to close. Ironically, that summer had been a good one for the East Coast. Eight thousand people a week had packed into Filey, but the site was in need of significant investment and the company just wasn't convinced it would be money well spent.

At Butlin's head office there was a feeling that the business had been damaged by the popular TV sitcom *Hi-De-Hi!* Written by David Croft and Jimmy Perry (Perry had been a Redcoat at the Pwllheli camp), the first episode had aired in 1980. Set in a fictional 1950s camp called Maplins, millions tuned in each week to see Croft and Perry poke fun at the collection of misfits who ran the place and the people who holidayed there.

'It didn't make any difference to the people who had visited Butlin's recently,' said the company's official statement. 'But it re-enacted all the wakey-wakey calls and regimentation of the early days.'

Perhaps, but Butlin's wasn't brought down by a sitcom. Its traditional holidaymakers had begun to look enviously at the Spanish Costas and the company itself was already attempting to replicate its offering abroad. When the end came under lowering clouds and a stiffish breeze, Filey was a picture of desolation. These were the days before slick human resources departments and the 101 permanent staff were told that morning to go home, have a cup of tea and think about their futures.

There would be no more stars beginning their careers on the stage of the Gaiety Theatre and no more holiday romances sparked thanks to a little Dutch courage served in the Beachcomber Bar. By the end of the day, leaves had already begun to settle on the outdoor pool and for the first time in more than forty years there was no one to clear them.

'Butlin's was a place where pretty much anything went,' says Tony Peers. 'It was a well-oiled machine and it was the place to learn about the entertainment business. Because we were with the holidaymakers all week they were a sympathetic crowd. Even if you were terrible, and most of us were in the early days, they would still chuckle along.

'Go there now and all that's left is the echo of long-forgotten laughter.'

Opposite: For those who wanted peace and quiet, Butlin's – where all guests were encouraged to take part in activities – was probably not for them.

BRIG

H T O N

In March 1968 there was more activity than usual on Brighton's West Pier. While a marching band, complete with bearskins, was going through one final rehearsal, a young Richard Attenborough was finalising the running order for that day's filming. *Oh, What a Lovely War!* was to be his directorial debut and he'd chosen the West Pier as one of the key locations for the musical satirising Britain's involvement in the First World War.

'It really did look like it was 1914,' remembers Mary Pratt, who was one of the many locals drafted in to help out on the production. 'Shop front signs had been changed and they'd covered up anything too modern. I was helping out on wardrobe. I was only seventeen and it was incredibly exciting to be a part of, plus the money was incredible. I was paid £30. To me that was an absolute fortune, although I'm not sure I spent it very wisely.'

By the time the film, starring Dirk Bogarde,

John Gielgud, Corin Redgrave and Maggie Smith among others, was released the following year, the pier was about to become the lead character in its own drama. It was one that would run for years and which would ultimately end in disaster for a town with a reputation as the elder statesman of Britain's seaside resorts.

From the extravagance of the Royal Pavilion, built for the Prince Regent, later King George IV, to the antiques shops of The Lanes, Brighton has always valued its past. That's why the creaking metal skeleton of what remains of the West Pier, once one of the grandest in the country and the only one ever to be Grade I listed, has become such a poignant symbol of what might have been.

Now stranded out to sea, it will eventually be reclaimed by the waves. Even the Trust, originally set up to campaign for its restoration, knows that there is no way back. The only thing it can do now is record

This page: Following the First World War, holidaymakers again returned to the coast. Photographed here in 1934, Brighton's pebble beach was always busy in summer.

Previous pages: Brighton's Palace Pier as seen from the Kings Road in the early twentieth century.

Right: Brighton's famous son, the entertainer Max Miller, began his career as principal entertainer on the West Pier.

Far Right: Stanley Watson became a professional magician after the Second World War. Along with his wife Diane, the couple performed regularly at Brighton.

While initially just a place to promenade and breathe in the best sea air, it wasn't long before the money men realised that, if they could also provide onsite entertainment, it would discourage their captive audience from spending money elsewhere.

the memories of those for whom the pier provided a backdrop to countless long summer days and pay tribute to the man who designed it.

When Eugenius Birch died in 1884 at the age of sixty-six, he had left his unmistakable mark on fourteen British seaside resorts. His journey round the coast had begun in Margate and taken in Scarborough, Aberystwyth and Eastbourne, before ending in Plymouth where his last pier was built the same year he died. However, Brighton was his undoubted masterpiece.

Birch had begun his career designing bridges and viaducts and when he returned from overseas, where he had been advising the East Indian Railway Company, he spotted an opportunity that was too good to miss. Back home, railways were also transforming the lives of ordinary people. Britain's middle classes were suddenly mobile, tourism was on the brink of an explosion and entrepreneurs were heading to the coast in the hope of finding their fortune on the sands. A number of piers had already

been built, but most were simple wooden affairs. Birch reckoned he could do better.

'He wasn't just an engineer and an architect,' says Brighton historian Fred Gray. 'He was an artist. Prior to Birch, piers had given people the unusual feeling of being at sea without the fear of getting wet or becoming seasick, but they had generally been quite plain. Birch had bigger plans. The West Pier at Brighton was one of the first to be built for promenading and would give successful Victorians a chance to show off their wealth. In those early days, piers were pretty much exclusively designed as an extension to the seafront for middle class families. They came to walk, they came to rest and while they came to breathe in healthy air, they also came to be seen.'

When the pier opened in 1866, one local MP described it poetically as 'a kind of butterfly upon the ocean to carry visitors upon its wings and waft them among the zephyrs and balmy breezes of Brighton'.

Certainly the six small buildings on top, designed by Birch in an Oriental style, seemed impossibly fashionable. As the resort's great and good became the very first to pass through the toll booths, walking on to the pier head where glass panels protected them from the wind and sun, they couldn't help but hope some of the glamour would rub off on them.

Ten years later, when the 1,115ft of planks were echoing to the tread of 600,000 people, the West Pier had cemented Brighton's reputation as a premier resort.

While initially just a place to promenade and breathe in the best sea air, it wasn't long before the money men realised that if they could also provide onsite entertainment, it would discourage their captive audience from spending money elsewhere. By the 1920s, the West Pier had its own concert hall, pavilion and a programme to rival the largest London theatres. Aside from regular performances from the pier's resident orchestra, led by the renowned conductor Lyell Taylor, the concert hall and theatre staged plays, ballets, military tattoos and provided the launch pad for the career of comedian Max Miller. Later known to millions as the Cheeky Chappie, Miller was talent-spotted by veteran Brighton entertainer Jack Sheppard. Delivering his first public performance on the beach in 1913, after just one season Miller, one of the first comedians

Opposite: The variety performers of the West Pier pose for a photograph on the beach during the final summer season in 1970.

This page: Song and dance troupes would pitch up on the beach close to the pier where they knew they would have a captive audience.

who set out to deliberately shock audiences, was promoted to the West Pier's principle entertainer.

His act wasn't to everyone's taste, but for anyone who thought him crass there were a dozen others who hung on his every word. Coming out on stage, he would wink at the gallery and ask the audience to choose between two books of jokes. One was white, the other blue. Invariably the blue book, containing lines like 'I went to a nudist camp the other day, when they sat down it was like a round of applause', won.

Miller's humour may not have been the most sophisticated, but it earned him a fortune and each time he drove past the West Pier in his Rolls-Royce with its glass roof, it was always a reminder of just how far he had come.

By the time Miller became the first British variety star to be paid more than £1,000 a week in 1943, Brighton's West Pier was also entering another golden age, one wealthy Londoners in particular were keen to be a part of. Every Friday evening, the *Brighton Belle* would be packed with those hoping to spot the town's famous faces, such as Laurence Olivier, at the next table and who eased their train

journey to the coast by ordering half-bottles of Chablis. The end of the war brought a renewed sense of optimism and a glut of performers, who had spent the previous six years boosting the morale of troops as part of the Entertainments National Service Association, better known as ENSA, in need of work.

One of them was magician Stanley Watson.

'I think he thought that after the war that would be the end of his career in show business,' says his wife, Kath. 'Stanley had been based out in the Far East and was among the last of the troops to be brought back. When he eventually arrived home all the decent jobs had gone, so he decided to carry on with his magic. At the time I was performing in a dance troupe and Stanley and I often ended up on the same bill. That's how we met and then one day he asked if I would like to be his assistant.'

The couple became regulars on the bill at the West Pier and both shared the belief that, whatever problems you had offstage, they had to be set aside once the curtain went up.

'I'd wear beautiful evening dresses and I even changed by name to Diane, thinking it sounded more

The decline of the West Pier was not obvious at first. When a nearby photographic studio started noticing that fewer people were stopping by for a souvenir picture, they put it down to poor weather.

Left: Brighton's West Pier fell into decline in the 1960s and by the end of the decade the cost of repairs had risen to almost £1m.

Opposite: In 2003, all hopes of restoring the pier went up in flames when a fire destroyed the iconic concert hall and pavilion.

sophisticated. The reality was that we were often staying in digs overrun with mice that liked the taste of greasepaint, but an audience wants to buy into a glamorous world and that's what we'd give them.'

Inventing most of his own tricks, Stanley's tribute to the Queen's Coronation in 1953 was one of those seen for the first time by West Pier audiences. Eating a series of light bulbs from a replica of the royal crown, once each one had been swallowed he would pause for a moment before the finale.

'Ah, yes,' says Kath, who played the glamorous assistant for more than thirty years. 'You could hear the gasps as he pulled them back out of his mouth, all lit up on a piece of string. Stanley was a real master of manipulation and sleight of hand.'

The West Pier might have emerged from the shadow of war a slightly more down-market version of its original self, but it was arguably more successful than ever before. It was where holidaymakers flocked to see Professor Conky Javin swaying gently on the end of a high-diving board. Handcuffed and wrapped in chains, when a suitable crowd had gathered, he would drop, without warning, into the waters below. Javin had been a

steward and a cook in the Navy before turning to escapology and he'd quickly learnt the art of keeping an audience hooked.

'Once you've hit the bottom and whipped the chains off it becomes boring,' he admitted to a reporter from *The Times* in 1951. 'Trouble is, you mustn't come up too quick. The public aren't interested unless they think you've drowned yourself. So you have to bide your time, walking about on the seabed. What I don't like are the silly beggars who dive in after you to save you – they don't half get annoyed when they find you walking around on the bottom.'

Javin, who supplemented his income by working as a cleaner in a nearby office block, was following in a long line of daredevil entertainers on the West Pier. Men like Albert Higgins Heppell who learnt the cost of pedalling his bicycle straight off a high platform and into the sea when, in 1912, he slipped and died from a fractured skull.

The decline of the West Pier was not obvious at first. When a nearby photographic studio started noticing that fewer people were stopping by for a souvenir picture, they put it down to poor weather;

when ticket sales began to fall at the theatre it was excused as a temporary blip.

It wasn't. By the late 1960s those who had once headed to Brighton were being tempted by fashionable resorts in the south of France and you were more likely to spot one of the Mad Dogs of Sussex, a dubious Brighton gang, wandering along the West Pier than any famous faces.

Neglected and half empty, the structure soon began to deteriorate. By the end of the decade it was reckoned the necessary repairs could run to almost £1 million. No one wanted the pier to go, but, equally, no one seemed to be able to find the money to save it and the 1970 summer show was the last.

'I've got very fond memories of that show,' says Kath, who, along with Stanley, who died in 2009, was among the last acts to perform at the West Pier theatre. 'Of course it was sad to think that was it for the West Pier, but we all wanted to give it the best send-off we could.'

Over the best part of three decades a succession of plans were unveiled to restore the pier and in 1982 it was Grade I listed by English Heritage. However, each time it seemed progress was being made, disaster would strike. In the late 1980s, just as the Brighton West Pier Trust was gathering momentum, two violent storms severed the structure from the land.

Worse was to come.

A decade later the Heritage Lottery Fund was set to throw the pier a lifeline, announcing a grant of more than £14 million. However, in 2003, before work had even got under way, part of the concert hall collapsed into the sea. When, the same year, two arson attacks destroyed the concert hall and pavilion, the money was withdrawn.

'It became an increasingly forlorn sight cut off from the land,' says Fred Gray. 'No longer a place of seaside fun, just a home for pigeons and starlings. There is no way back now. All we can do is watch and wait for the day when the final remains of this once great pier disappear under the waves for ever.'

This page: The skeleton of Brighton's famous pier has long stood as a reminder of the golden age of the Great British seaside.

MABLET

THORPE

In September 1966, Percy Harrison became the country's biggest ever winner of the Football Pools, pocketing a cheque for £338,356. His win also proved to be the best advertisement for Mablethorpe the resort had enjoyed in years.

Posing for the cameras, the fifty-two-year-old, who had never been to a football match and who had only played the Pools once before, was asked how he planned to spend his newly acquired fortune. Standing alongside Maud, his wife of thirty years, like many couples who come into an unexpected windfall he talked of buying a new house, of giving his five children a slice of the pot and perhaps spending a little on a dream holiday. Pressed on the details, Percy, who had been earning £14 a week in a fertiliser factory, said: 'We are going to travel because it broadens the mind. But we shan't leave England. The furthest I've ever been before today is Cleethorpes and that was bad enough.' Maud, who used to earn a little extra holiday money picking potatoes, agreed. 'I know we can go anywhere in the world,' she added. 'But the place I'd most like to go is Mablethorpe. It's lovely.'

Tourism chiefs in the Lincolnshire resort hadn't been so excited since D.H. Lawrence chose Mablethorpe as the holiday destination of the Morel family in *Sons and Lovers* more than half a century earlier.

It also couldn't have come at a better time. Campaigners were two years into a protracted battle to save the railway line which had turned Mablethorpe

from a sleepy agricultural place into a fashionable seaside resort, described in one late nineteenth-century guide as 'quite a paradise for children; so perfectly safe that they can paddle to their hearts content and go about barefoot all day long'.

When it opened in the 1870s, the railway had connected the flat plains of Lincolnshire to the rest of the country. While the area's many farmers had seen it purely as a way of getting their produce out to a much wider customer base, it also opened up the region's holiday industry. Believed to be the only station in the country with its own windmill to pump the water needed for the steam engines, soon carriages packed with families craving sea air were pulling into this small corner of the east coast.

'Without the railways there wouldn't be holiday resorts as we know them,' says Russell Hollowood, associate curator of collections at York's National Railway Museum. 'Initially the big rail companies thought trains would just take the cream of the stagecoach traffic. It was a fairly inflexible service, so much so that the timetables were cast in metal because they never thought they were going to change. However, it wasn't long before they realised that you could pack a lot of people into an old coal train. That was really the start of what we think of now as the Great British holiday. Most of these excursion trains would leave early in the morning and then return late at night. People were squeezed in, so it wasn't a

Previous pages: The arrival of the railway in the 1870s transformed Mablethorpe from a sleepy coastal town into a thriving seaside resort.

Left: Mablethorpe didn't have a grand theatre or a large swimming stadium, but it marketed itself as a destination for wholesome family holidays.

Opposite: Holiday brochures from the 1950s and 1960s, produced by British Railways, promoted the resort's golden sands and good value accommodation.

MABLETHORPE
AND SUTTON-ON-SEA

Illustrated guide free from Publicity Manager, Mablethorpe

Train services and fares from **BRITISH RAILWAYS** stations, offices and agencies

The Dunes Theatre, Mablethorpe.

Left: In 1947, Mablethorpe added an open air theatre to its list of attractions. Nestled behind the promenade it was only closed to the elements in 1960s.

Once the preserve of the wealthy, the seaside was now accessible to ordinary families and when they got to resorts like Mablethorpe they wanted to experience everything else the middle and upper classes had enjoyed.

particularly pleasant travel experience, but it was still a trip to the seaside and the demand was incredible.

'Suddenly in previously quiet towns you had hundreds of people descending all wanting places to eat and drink. It took a lot of places by surprise. We have this image of those first Victorian holidaymakers as being rather staid, but actually that wasn't the case. There are lots of reports of working-class men arriving at the coast, stripping off and diving into the water. You can see why. They spent their lives in the dirt and noise of heavy industry. Suddenly they got to the coast and here was this great expanse of water: who wouldn't have wanted to dive in?'

Once the preserve of the wealthy, the seaside was now accessible to ordinary families and when they got to resorts like Mablethorpe they wanted to experience everything else the middle and upper classes had enjoyed.

'It's the reason why donkey rides started,' says Russell. 'The working classes wanted to try horse riding and donkeys were the next best thing. The railways changed the atmosphere of many resorts and, if you'd ask some, not always for the better. There were those who felt this new influx of holidaymakers was out of control. The success of the railways led to a wave of moral panic and eventually the introduction of male- and female-segregated beaches.'

While tourism was put on hold during the Great War, by 1921 railway companies were in a position to restore tourist tickets for the next holiday season. Valid for two months, the scheme allowed passengers to enjoy 'go as you please' holidays, breaking the journey at any station. For small resorts like Mablethorpe it proved a boon, attracting those who might not have wanted to stay a week, but who were quite happy to idle away a couple of days before moving on to somewhere else.

David Lascelles remembers it well. When his family first moved to Mablethorpe in the 1940s they bought a grocery and general store and when the summer holidays began he spotted a business opportunity of his own.

Above: On 1 February, 1953, Mablethorpe was left underwater when the whole of the East Coast was hit by one of the worst storms in living memory.

Left: David Lascelles (third from left) made the most of growing up in Mablethorpe, acting as a porter for the holidaymakers who arrived by train.

'The working classes wanted to try horse riding and donkeys were the next best thing. The railways changed the atmosphere of many resorts and, if you'd ask some, not always for the better.'

'The station was where it was at. You can't believe now how many people would pour out on to the platform. Saturday was the day for new arrivals. There was no real taxi service in those days, so me and a few friends would head up there and see if anyone wanted help with their luggage. We'd wheel our big wooden barrows on to the platform and I don't remember ever leaving empty-handed. Suitcases were great big heavy things and no one had yet thought of adding wheels to the bottom. We'd load up our barrows and off we'd go. It was really hard work, but we needed the money and if you picked the right family they'd give you a good tip.'

Dave supplemented his income as a porter with beachcombing. Mablethorpe's old Victorian sea defences were a magnet for holidaymakers, who would inevitably lose something down the slats, as they spent the day sunbathing on the wooden boards.

'Watches, rings, coins all ended up in the sand below. Most didn't even notice they'd gone and, even if they did, they didn't know how to get them back. We spent years engineering various different implements, but the best was probably a length of bamboo with a teaspoon strapped to the end.'

Mablethorpe's lack of pretension was what attracted many holidaymakers, but it was also the cause of some irritation among those who lived just a few miles down the road. Sutton-on-Sea was inclined to look down its nose at its neighbour, a tendency beautifully illustrated in the summer of 1955 in a row over public art. The previous winter a statue of an amply proportioned mermaid had been erected at Sutton-on-Sea. Bearing more than a passing resemblance to Marilyn Monroe, there had been reports of men secretly taking pictures of it when their wives weren't looking, and when more sensitive souls found themselves walking past the mermaid they kept their eyes fixed to the ground. Amid a flurry of letters of complaint, Sutton-on-Sea councillor D.E. Mayfield said what many others had been thinking.

'We cater for family visitors, the good type. When the mermaid appeared everyone was up in arms. It's repulsive. It's not so bad at night, but in the day it's a shocker. It will be all right for Mablethorpe, that's the sort of thing they want.'

The response of Mablethorpe councillor Alice Fowler was typical of a town always happy to give the thousands who filed out of its station each summer all the trappings of a British seaside resort:

'You can eat fish and chips in the paper here and no one bats an eyelid … And what's nicer than a young shapely figure. There are far more repulsive figures on the beach.'

So taken was Mablethorpe with the mermaid that they later adopted her as the symbol of the town. It may not have had a grand tower like Blackpool or an impressive pier like the Brightons and Great Yarmouths of this world, but for those who demanded from their holiday little more than a sandy beach, a dip in the sea and somewhere comfortable and inexpensive to rest their head for the night, Mablethorpe did the job.

During the 1950s the number of passengers disembarking each year at the town's station had risen from 124,000 at the start of the decade to 136,400 by the end. Many had been attracted by the London and North Eastern Railway's iconic railway posters. Designed by artist Donald F. Blake, he borrowed the 'children's paradise' tagline and showed the sands and open-air pool packed with families.

'Competition between the big four railway companies had really begun to increase and the tourism market had become much more sophisticated,' says Russell Hollowood. 'The first dual carriageway had been built in Britain in the 1930s. Not only was car ownership rising, but the charabancs, those early form of coach trips, were proving increasingly popular.

'Early rail posters had been very basic and very text heavy, but by this period they had really embraced the art of advertising and they spent a lot of money employing some of the best artists in the country to produce these now iconic posters.'

The holidaymakers had kept on coming and, given the events of 1953, it was easy to see why Mablethorpe thought itself unbeatable.

On 1 February that year, along with most settlements along the East Coast, Mablethorpe was hit by one of the worst storms the country had ever seen. In the early hours of the morning, 45ft waves, rolling before an 80mph gale, smashed into sea defences, sweeping scores of people to their deaths and battering down houses as if they had been made of paper. The coastguard, shouting to make himself heard above the gale, telephoned through a warning.

'The waves,' he said, 'are smashing the sea wall to hell.' Within minutes, seawater had roared into the

Step forward Dr Richard Beeching. It was on 27 March 1963 that he went public with his report called The Reshaping of British Railways. It was a rather innocuous title for what would turn out to be brutal changes to the network. Mablethorpe was among the losers.

streets and almost a million tonnes of sand, which lay like deep snowdrifts had buried everything in its path.

'Mablethorpe was practically written off,' remembers Dave, who, along with the rest of the population, was evacuated as squads of police officers were brought in to prevent the looting of the town's 1,800 bungalows. 'You can understand why. The place looked as though it had been obliterated, but no one who lived here was prepared to let the town die. As soon as they could, the guesthouse owners and those who ran the attractions came back to clean up.'

The storm may have taken less than an hour to destroy a town built over decades, but within two years it was almost impossible to see where the damage had been done. Covering a visit by the Duke of Edinburgh to mark the second anniversary of the disaster, *The Times* noted, 'the greatest achievement is perhaps in regaining an air of quiet respectability, as of a place where nothing more serious happens than the last shower of rain'.

Mablethorpe had fought back from the brink, but another battle was looming which would inflict more pain on the resort than any act of God.

Step forward Dr Richard Beeching. It was on 27 March 1963 that he went public with his report called *The Reshaping of British Railways*. It was a rather innocuous title for what would turn out to be brutal changes to the network. Mablethorpe was among the losers. When the line between the resort and Louth had closed three years earlier after running at a substantial loss there had been reassurances that a second line, running inland to Willoughby and used mainly by tourists, would be preserved. Dr Beeching showed no such consideration. The civil servant had been asked to look at the country's creaking rail network and concluded that all unprofitable lines would have to go, among them the route which for more than seventy years had been ferrying holidaymakers to and from the coast. There was some justification. Car ownership was on the up, but thousands of families living on modest wages, the kind who holidayed in places like Mablethorpe, were still largely reliant on public transport. If they couldn't catch a train to one seaside resort, they would simply go to another.

'It's true that the statistics used for the report were taken during April and obviously didn't reflect summer holiday traffic,' says Russell. 'However, it's also true that it was uneconomical to have rolling stock, which was only used for a couple of months, sat idle for the rest of the year. Of course there are persuasive arguments about why it's better to take people off the roads, why it's important to ensure outlying places are connected by rail, but that wasn't Dr Beeching's brief. He was brought in to look solely at the bottom line.'

A campaign group was formed and under continued pressure British Rail appeared to do a U-turn. Mablethorpe would not only keep its railway, but it would also look to boost holiday traffic on the line. The promise proved an empty one. Over the next few years those who had fought to save the service watched as it was quietly run into the ground. Cheap tickets, which had once lured holidaymakers to Mablethorpe, were withdrawn and the timetable reduced. By the winter of 1969, British Rail had issued an ultimatum. It had been given government approval to close the line unless the authorities in Lincolnshire could offer financial support. The stay of execution lasted ten months. With no offer forthcoming, the axe finally fell on 3 October 1970. When the last train pulled out of Mablethorpe onboard were five hundred passengers and two coffins, a visible symbol of the ending of an era.

Today the site of Mablethorpe's old railway belongs to the Station Sports Centre. Nothing is left of the waiting rooms or the ticket office, but in the grounds you can still see the remains of the platform where Dave Lascelles would tout for business each Saturday during July and August.

'It sometimes feels like it's been airbrushed out of history,' he says. 'The railway transformed this place, but overnight we went right back to square one.'

Opposite above: Mablethorpe's tourism industry relied on daytrippers, who took advantage of cheap train tickets to the coast.

Opposite below: In Mablethorpe everything stopped for the resort's donkeys, including the traffic, as the animals made their way to the beach.

H A S T

I N G S

On a hill above Hastings there's a cluster of ordinary looking houses. Few aside from Richard Pitcairn-Knowles would bother to look twice at the development.

'There's not much to see,' he admits. 'You can just about make out the old stable block, but everything else went. Every so often my conscience will be occasionally pricked by the thought we should have done more to save the old place, but it wasn't to be.'

The buildings he talks of belonged to Riposo Health Hydro. Founded by Richard's grandfather, Andrew, and later run by his father, Gordon, the retreat was born out of the same idea which had seen crowds flocking to Scarborough in the eighteenth century in search of fresh sea air and the resort's healing spa waters.

'For a long time in Britain, bathing was something to be disapproved of,' says Ian D. Rotherham, a professor of environmental geography and reader in tourism at Sheffield Hallam University. 'It was linked to religion and the idea that the more physical deprivation you endured the better your spiritual credentials. However, gradually attitudes towards health and cleanliness changed and many of the spa towns, so important to the Romans, suddenly became fashionable again. Initially those who visited spas were both wealthy and educated and

it remained an upper class pursuit really until the Industrial Revolution created a new urban middle class who really embraced the supposed health benefits of drinking and bathing in spa waters. Originally it was thought that to get the best results treatments had to take place *in situ*, but by the end of the Victorian period all that had changed. Many seaside resorts without their own springs began opening their hydro hotels boasting a range of exotic treatments borrowed from the spa towns of Eastern Europe.'

It was in 1912, the same year Lord Chichester announced he was selling off the ruins of Hastings Castle, where William the Conqueror had stayed before the infamous battle of 1066, that Andrew Pitcairn-Knowles also entered the Hastings property market.

Ridgecroft didn't have the same historic associations as the ancient castle ruins just a few miles down the road, but the five-bedroom, three-storey Victorian house and its extensive grounds would soon have its own claim to fame. Named after the Italian word for rest, Riposo was about to become the first hydro in England to promote what was known in Europe as the Nature Cure. Within the thirty or so chalets and the various treatment rooms guests would spend their days lying in baths covered

Previous pages: By 1936, when this photograph was taken, previously unflattering and practical swimwear had been given a makeover. The more flattering designs helped spark a raft of seaside bathing beauty competitions.

Opposite: Andrew Pitcairn-Knowles believed exercise was a key to keeping healthy, long before the keep-fit craze arrived in Britain.

Right: At Riposo, treatment began from the feet up, with guests encouraged to spend a few minutes each morning walking barefoot on the grass.

in blankets, expelling toxins, aided, they hoped, by a wholly vegetarian diet. When the weather allowed, the regime would be supplemented by daily exercise classes on the lawn and nude sunbathing.

However, only the most determined signed up to Riposo's signature treatment. The Schroth Cure could last for anything from six days to ten weeks and for the most part it involved fasting, save for the odd bread roll, and avoiding liquids apart from a bottle of wine prescribed every couple of days.

'It never felt like a peculiar place to grow up,' recalls Richard, who later trained as an osteopath. 'I was born at Riposo and that was all I knew. I remember when I met my wife, she thought I was quite odd both for my choice of career and the fact I was vegetarian. I suspect I might have been neither had it not be for my upbringing.'

Prior to turning his attention to the business of health at the age of thirty-nine, Andrew Pitcairn-Knowles had been a successful photojournalist. Specialising in sport, he'd always been interested in fitness and, having spent most of his life living in Europe he admired the way the Germans, Austrians and Italians embraced outdoor pursuits. However, had his young son, Gordon, not been kicked in the stomach by a mule, Andrew might well have been content to stay behind the lens.

The incident happened while the family was staying in Corsica, but in the belief that the best

medical treatment was in Germany, Gordon was soon transferred to Berlin.

What Andrew witnessed in the German capital would change his family's life for ever. While in Britain doctors may have recommended bed rest and regular doses of vitamin-packed tonics, in Berlin Gordon was subject to a myriad of treatments.

So convinced was Andrew by the approach that when his young son was fully recovered he embarked on a tour of Continental spa resorts. Taking detailed notes of all the treatments on offer, and the kind of facilities needed to attract the right clientele, he formed a plan and headed back to Britain in search of a suitable property. He found it in Hastings, already an established and popular resort. Down by the pier, the various theatres and guesthouses were already catering for those who came to the coast looking for escapism. Riposo would cater for those who believed breathing in the sea air, while enjoying some of the latest treatments from the Continent, would cure their various ailments.

'The craze had begun in the Victorian age,' explains Dr Rotherham. 'Diseases like consumption, typhus and cholera had taken huge tolls in many industrial towns. People were desperate for cures and often the more drastic and unpleasant the treatment the more likely people were persuaded of its benefits.

'Whenever a new scientific discovery was made, there was a tendency to attach a health benefit to it

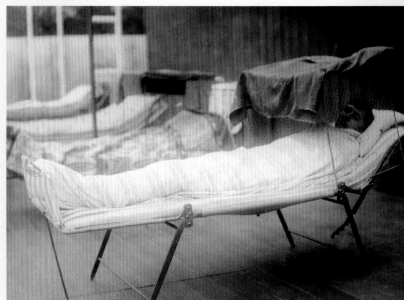

and so it was with electricity and radiation. Electrotherapy, where people had currents passed through them as they sat in baths of hot water or mud, became incredibly popular and radiation was hailed as a miracle cure for all sorts of ailments. Knowing what we know now it seems ludicrous, but it wasn't until those working with radioactive substances began to die that people started to realise that some of the more outlandish claims didn't have much basis in fact.'

There was no radiation treatment at Riposo, but the naturopathy favoured by the Pitcairn-Knowles family was nevertheless guided by a no pain, no gain philosophy.

Based on the idea that all diseases are the result of poisons in the body, its early advocates insisted there was no point simply treating the symptoms of gout, asthma or arthritis. The root cause had to be addressed and, caught early enough, they believed a whole raft of conditions could be alleviated, even cured, by a programme of treatments designed to rid the body of toxins.

At Riposo, guests might begin the day walking barefoot over the dewy grass outside their chalet. Afterwards, if the weather was fine, it was often recommended they spent twenty minutes or so in a sun box, changing position every five minutes or so to ensure every part of their body was exposed to the rays. Finally, the afternoon might revolve around one of the various hydrotherapy treatments, like

the cabinet bath where guests would sit with their head poking out of the top while steam was passed through the wooden box. In another room there was what looked like a tunnel filled with light bulbs. The resort's medical staff called it the electric light bath and the dry heat it produced was said to be good for the joints. To break the treatment cycle, every so often Andrew would muster as many cars as he could for a paper chase across the countryside, and on Thursdays he would book seats for the latest show at the Bexhill Pavilion. However, come the morning, socks were once again removed as Riposo's guests began slowly pacing the grounds hoping they were curing themselves from the feet up.

'I know it all sounds slightly bizarre these days, but you have to remember that when Riposo was established antibiotics were still nearly fifty years away, anaesthetics were little advanced from chloroform, and transplant surgery was still science fiction,' says Richard. 'So, yes, some of the treatments sound heroic, laughable even, but many of them filled the gap between the medicine of the nineteenth and that of the later twentieth century.

'There has never been any real scientific research into why these methods apparently improved the health of so many people. However, the immune system, hormone system and nervous system are all delicately balanced and integrated, so it's not surprising that they become disturbed by poor diet,

little exercise and lack of sleep. My own theory is that it probably wasn't just a placebo effect. The treatment at Riposo was a bit like allowing a fire to go out, clearing the grate and starting again.'

A few weeks after our conversation, Richard calls to point me in the direction of a new study from the University of Southern California claiming fasting, even for as little as three days, may increase the production of white blood cells and help rejuvenate the immune system. There may have been something in the Schroth Cure after all.

One element of the regime compulsory to all guests was a meat-free diet. While vegetarianism wasn't exactly mainstream, it had already found support within the temperance movement of the early nineteenth century and the first vegetable diet cook book had been published in 1832 by Martha Brotherton, wife of the Salford MP Joseph Brotherton.

By 1847, the Vegetarian Society was up and running and the movement gained high-profile backing from the likes of bakery magnate Dr Thomas Richard Allinson, shorthand guru Isaac Pitman and playwright George Bernard Shaw. While Britain remained very much a meat and two veg nation, by the time Andrew Pitcairn-Knowles had established

Riposo's kitchen garden to provide most of the ingredients for the guests' meals, the idea of a diet without pork chops, shepherd's pie and beef stew and dumplings wasn't just fanciful thinking.

'We ate salad. A lot of salad, interspersed with the odd nut cutlet,' says Richard, who has published a recipe book of Riposo's favourite vegetarian dishes. 'They took diet very seriously. My father in particular was a great animal lover and hated the idea of unnecessary suffering, so much so that when the large compost pit at the bottom of the garden became overrun with rats he was left in a bit of a quandary. He disliked the idea of poisoning them, fearing it would cause them a long and painful death, so instead he either lay in wait for them with a twelve-bore shotgun or, after catching them in traps, would release the rats on to the croquet lawn where several male members of staff, armed with clubs, were lined up. In my father's thinking they would either be killed by a single fatal blow or would be lucky enough to escape unharmed.'

While some health resorts boasted exclusivity, Riposo always traded on a reputation of affordability. Fees for accommodation were comparatively modest and the hydro's doors were open to all, including, in

Opposite: The treatment programme at Riposo was designed to rid the body of toxins and as well as promoting a vegetarian diet, it included sessions in cabinet baths, where steam was passed through a specially constructed box, and being wrapped in hot towels.

Right: The occultist Aleister Crowley was a guest at Riposo, booking in for a number of treatments in 1945 when he was staying at a nearby guesthouse.

Left: She was the ultimate sex symbol, which is perhaps why a Hastings beauty contest in 1958 went in search of a seaside Marilyn Monroe.

Opposite: Away from Riposo, holidaymakers could enjoy more traditional seaside entertainment, like these clowns performing in the summer carnival of 1956.

1945, Aleister Crowley. The man who was variously described as a mystic, occultist, ceremonial magician, deviant and recreational drug user, but who most knew simply as The Beast, was seventy years old and in failing health. He'd been staying in a nearby guesthouse, where the owners had described him as perfectly pleasant, and came to Riposo for a little rest and relaxation.

The records don't show what treatment Crowley had or whether he enjoyed his stay, but as he lay on one of the beds, staring up at the ceiling, he may well have noticed a few cracks beginning to appear in the old building.

Riposo was in need of investment, but a significant slice of the family fortune had been lost during the Second World War and money for repairs was tight. When Andrew died in 1956 at the age of eighty-eight, Gordon did his best to keep the place running. However, when he was diagnosed with terminal lung cancer just a few years later, it was the beginning of the end. As his condition deteriorated, in 1962 Riposo closed and when Gordon died the following year the family faced some tough decisions.

'When they were first opened, the chalets with their gas fires had a cosy kind of charm, but as the years went on guests demanded more and more and there just wasn't enough money to pay for it,' says Richard. 'We decided there was no option but to sell up. Andrew's wife Margaret,

who had supported him 100 per cent, watched the demolition and that must have been heartbreaking. Riposo represented half a century of work, but it disappeared in just a few days.'

A similar fate had already befallen many of Britain's other hydros and today it's as though the industry, still strong in countries like the Czech Republic and Germany, never existed at all on these shores.

'When I was younger, I just saw Grandfather as an old man and it was only in later years that I realised what a forward-thinking chap he was and much of what he was recommending all those years ago is now part of mainstream thinking,' says Richard, who ran what he swears will be his last London Marathon at the age of eighty in 2013. 'We are told to cut down on the amount of red meat we eat, we are told to eat more vegetables. If you ever needed an advert for the benefits of a raw food diet then you only had to look at Riposo's Dr Latto. He was forever taking photographs of himself halfway up a mountainside looking twenty years younger than he actually was.

'I wish it could have survived, but the kind of treatments it offered just fell out of fashion in this country. I think there's also something in the fact that the pace of life was beginning to change. Some of the treatments we offered lasted up to six weeks and they could because life was a lot less hurried back then. The pace of life changed and sadly Riposo just wasn't able to keep up.'

H O R

N S E A

It's a winter's morning at the coast and while one man and his dog make the most of the beautifully desolate sands, it seems the rest of Hornsea has decamped to one of the various cafés lining the high street.

Just up the road, the town's museum is closed for the season and repeated knocking is met with silence. Press your nose to the window and it looks like one of those typically quaint museums Britain does so well. The gift shop has an eclectic range of souvenirs sitting alongside information leaflets penned by local historians and in place of hi-tech interactive attractions are mannequins and information boards. Eventually, Carol Harker unbolts the large wooden door apologising for the delay. She's been out the back sorting through the museum's extensive stores of Hornsea Pottery.

It was pottery which turned this otherwise unremarkable town into a destination resort and ultimately it was the demise of the factory which almost overnight pushed Hornsea back into the shadows.

'Hornsea Pottery put this little town on the map, it's as simple as that,' says Carol who volunteers at the museum. She's responsible for the 2,000 pieces of pottery in its collection and on days like this she can't help wondering what might have been. 'It was the heart and soul of this place. One of my first jobs was selling Hornsea Pottery. Everyone who grew up either worked there or knew someone who did, it was that kind of place. Sometimes now I think that people forget we're even here.'

Carol reaches for a collection of photographs showing the promenade gently heaving with holidaymakers and another of the Floral Hall, which used to extend its auditorium by opening the doors and creating alfresco stalls with deckchairs.

They were taken long before the pottery made its mark on the town in the 1950s, but, as Carol says, Hornsea wasn't the kind of resort to make brash statements of intent. Rather, it had always been content to go quietly about its business.

While other coastal towns demanded record-breaking piers, grand hotels and imposing concert halls, Hornsea didn't go in for those kinds of landmarks. Instead it had Rose Carr, a woman whose stature and reputation was equal to the work of even the most talented architect.

The railway had arrived in this genteel town in 1864 and Rose had followed six years later, taking over a local livery stables and trap hire. Standing

Previous pages: Hornsea's sands were once packed with holidaymakers from May to September.

Above: The Floral Hall was the resort's main centre of entertainment, with many watching summer concerts from the comfort of deckchairs.

Left: Minidale at Hornsea Pottery had everything a traditional village could boast, including a church, school and country pub.

This page: Hornsea was a genteel resort and with a large mere, described itself as the coastal equivalent of the Lake District.

outside the railway station with the other horse and carriage drivers waiting to meet the holidaymakers arriving on the train from Hull, she was impossible to miss. First there was her face. It had been left badly disfigured after she had been kicked in the face by a horse or possibly a cow. Anyone less confident might have tried to disguise their injuries. Not Rose.

While her trademark long black skirt and white apron were ordinary enough, the hat decorated with artificial flowers and the men's boots, which, like their owner, were best described as sturdy, meant she rarely blended into the background.

As those early visitors disembarked at Hornsea heading for the cottages they had rented from fishermen who would spend their summers under canvas on the beach, it wasn't long before they were being entertained with stories of Rose's legendary strength. Her 5ft 6in frame carried an impressive 19st 5lb and she could apparently lift sixteen sacks of corn or eighteen barrels of beer without breaking sweat. She was also the unofficial moral guardian of this small East Coast town. The tale of how she dunked a Hull City footballer in a horse trough after his language turned as blue as his lips following a bracing seaside training session was met with quiet approval.

Hornsea had no desire to be a Blackpool or a Margate. While the local press described the nearby working-class resort of Withernsea as 'stern and wild', Hornsea had a 'more quiet subdued air' and that's the way the local dignitaries wanted to keep it. By the turn of the twentieth century, railway posters by the likes of Charles W. Loten and the East Coast's own marine artist Harry Hudson Rodmell were dubbing Hornsea, with its large mere, 'Lakeland by the Sea', while tourist guides talked of delightful afternoon teas and praised the concert programme in the Floral Hall.

The chances are that Hornsea would have remained a refined but unremarkable resort had it not been for two brothers who embarked on the kind of enterprise any sensible financial adviser would have said was doomed to fail. It was in 1949 that Desmond Rawson and his younger brother Colin decided, quite out of the blue, to start a pottery in the small terraced house they shared in Victoria Avenue.

There were just two problems. Hornsea might have boasted a wide promenade, a summer carnival and touring circuses, but it neither had a ready supply of clay nor fuel to fire the kilns. The Rawsons, however, were not easily deterred and in the place of experience came boundless enthusiasm.

Desmond, who had lost two fingers while fighting in the Second World War, had learnt to model clay as part of his rehabilitation. He and Colin had also attended art school and, having secured some investment from a local businessman, they arranged for clay to be transported from Stoke-on-Trent and bought a secondhand gas-fired kiln. While the temperature in the house during the firing process was so high that it regularly caused the butter in their pantry to melt, production of Toby-style jugs and small vases began in earnest.

The Rawsons did not look back. A year later they took on their first employee, a sixteen-year-old called Mike Walker. That teenager is now in his seventies. He still lives nearby and came to know more than anyone what the pottery did for Hornsea.

'I'd just left school and I really didn't have a clue what to do. One day my father came home with a newspaper tucked under his arm. I remember he thrust it towards me and said, "Here's a job for you". There was an advertisement for Hornsea Pottery and it said they wanted an artistic and ambitious youth. To be honest I wasn't sure that I fitted the description, but I got on my bike in Beverley, about thirteen miles from Hornsea, and went to have a look.

'Desmond wasn't around when I got to the pottery,

Above: John Clappison, one of the early designers at Hornsea Pottery, was responsible for some of the company's most iconic ranges.

Right: The Rawson brothers began their pottery business in a small terraced house in 1949, using just one second-hand kiln.

Opposite: Hornsea Pottery not only became a major employer, but it also emerged as a tourist attraction with visitors keen to see the craftsmen at work.

Left: Desmond Rawson (left) and his brother, Colin, examine one of their products at Hornsea Pottery in April 1970.

Hornsea wasn't the kind of resort to make brash statements of intent. Rather, it had always been content to go quietly about its business.

so Colin gave me half a crown and told me to go and get a bit of lunch. When Desmond got back, he gave me a quick interview and then said, "When can you start?" I said, "What about next Monday". He said, "What's wrong with tomorrow?" I started the next day.'

The pottery would soon become central to the fortunes of the resort, but in those early years, as he busied himself sponging marks off the unbaked clay pots, the young apprentice didn't quite share the vision of its owners whom all the staff politely called Mr Desmond and Mr Colin.

'After a couple of years I had to go off to do my National Service with the RAF and I asked to stay on an extra year because I just wasn't convinced that there would be a job for me back home.'

By the time he did arrive back in East Yorkshire, Hornsea Pottery had moved into an old brick works on the edge of town and the large operation needed a trainee manager. Mike found himself back at the heart of the business which was fast becoming a tourist attraction in its own right.

'There'd often be a knock at the door and a group of people would be stood asking if they could have a look round. We didn't mind, it was flattering that people were interested, but if I wasn't free I would have to pull one of the men away from what they were doing.

'At first it didn't matter so much, but when word got round that the pottery was open to the public we were inundated.'

It was then that Mike suggested to the brothers that either they would have to ban all impromptu tours or employ an official guide. Reluctant to turn potential customers away, Colin agreed to take on another member of staff and set up a small shop selling rejects for half price. It wasn't long before ceramic teapots and biscuit barrels were being carefully packed in suitcases alongside the sticks of rock and shell-covered souvenirs.

'Hornsea always prided itself on quality – we even employed one woman whose sole job was to paint eyes on pottery bunny rabbits – and any piece which didn't meet our high standards never left the factory. I don't know what made me do it, but one day I spotted a pile of undecorated plates. For one reason or another they had failed the quality test, so I stuck

some pattern transfers on a batch of thirty or forty and took them over to the seconds shop. They flew off the shelves.

'I went to find Desmond, showed him one of the plates and asked what he thought of it. "Terrible," he said, but when I told him how many we'd just sold and for what price, he soon changed his mind. We were in business. I'll never forget as I went to leave he stopped me and asked if I needed the plate. I shook my head. "Leave it there," he said, "my mother-in-law will like it".'

As the pottery flourished so did the resort. While it still fiercely guarded its respectability – in the 1970s proposals to give 50 yards of Hornsea's sands over to those who wished to sunbathe nude following calls from the British Naturism Society sent local councillors into a spin – as a resort for families looking for simple pleasures, Hornsea had everything.

There was the Jiffy Bar, where the menu never changed and where the kitchen staff always ensured the place lived up to its name by serving every order in a jiffy; clocks could be set by Thorpe's Donkeys as they zig-zagged down the cliff path to the beach each morning and returned the same way at night; and the pottery had even developed its own theme park.

The falconry displays, adventure playground and go-kart circuit ensured the crowds, some 5,000-strong on the busiest days, would linger a little longer in Hornsea. In 1973, the pottery added another attraction when the model village known as Minidale welcomed its first visitors.

Designed by Geoffrey Cooper, who had first been inspired to create a world in miniature following a visit to the Bekonscot model village in Buckinghamshire, he had dedicated years to refining his skills in a draughty workshop underneath the railway arches in Hull.

'I gave up drinking and girls for two years,' he says, admitting Hornsea was the cause of some of his happiest and later most painful memories. 'On evenings and weekends I'd be down there making moulds and experimenting with different materials. It was a testing time, but I wanted to show anyone who had ever doubted me that I could do this.'

Geoffrey soon found a champion in Colin Rawson. 'He was a gentleman, a real gentleman. Minidale was a brilliant success, we were rated among the top ten attractions in Yorkshire. We had churches with stained-glass windows, a castle complete with a drawbridge and turrets, schools, pubs and more than a thousand figures. It was a work of art and for me a real labour of love.'

Those who had time to stroll leisurely through those tiny streets would be rewarded by spotting characters from *Last of the Summer Wine* and *Coronation Street*, and Geoffrey soon came to recognise the sound of laughter when someone discovered the small boy he'd placed on the miniature harbour side happily using the sea as an outdoor toilet.

From the Whitsun bank holiday to the first week in September there was a constant stream of tours through the factory and those same visitors would often stay to enjoy the model village, the boating lakes and Carlo Prati's Italian ice cream parlour.

As Carol Harker admits now, 'No one ever stopped to think what would happen if the pottery wasn't there.'

The beginning of the end came in 1984. The pottery was sold and it was to be the first in a series of painful takeovers. Mike found his services were no longer needed. He went to work for another pottery firm in Bridlington and, while there's no trace of bitterness about the way he was treated, the only physical reminder he has of the thirty-odd years he spent as manager are the two pottery giraffes belonging to his mother.

Soon quality was sacrificed in the hunt for greater margins. Cheap foreign competition was in part to blame, but when the factory began churning out the kind of tableware sold in any old discount store no one wanted a tour of the factory any more. With the once busy car park empty, Geoffrey also struggled to make a living from the model village. When the factory closed its doors in April 2000, the sadness was punctured by relief that this once great name had finally been put out of its misery.

The site is now the Freeport shopping village, the only reminder of its past life the street sign – Potters Way – leading to the cluster of designer stores and discount outlets.

'The problem is that people don't have time to stop and stare any more,' says Geoffrey. He moved some of his models to another site, but the rest were left to the elements as the site a thousand youngsters had once loved became overgrown. 'In the rush for new things we sacrificed a lot of what was good about the old days.'

S O U T H

PORT

In the early hours of the morning of 29 June 1927 a group of astronomers began to scale the Water Chute in Southport's Pleasureland.

The ride had been the first of its kind in any British resort when it opened in 1903, but that day no one was interested in plunging into the waters below. To the party of scientists, silhouetted in the moonlight, the Water Chute was just a convenient viewing platform from where they hoped to witness a total eclipse of the sun.

It had last been seen some 203 years earlier and, as they carefully positioned their telescopes on the wooden decking, they also had a bird's eye view of the crowds gathering below.

Using every possible form of transport, half a million people had travelled to the North West for the event that would not be seen again until the summer of 1999. There wasn't a room in the town free. Bed and breakfasts, reluctant to turn away paying guests, had turned bathrooms into bedrooms, while the big hotels were even offering armchairs for rent.

The crowds had begun to gather just after nightfall and as the yellow sands became black with cars, those astronomers standing on the Water Chute could just about hear the music playing from the gramophones below. The eclipse lasted for just 22.6 seconds, bathing the town momentarily in what one eyewitness described as a 'ghostly and unearthly light'. Like many of Pleasureland's rides, it might have been short but it was also exhilarating.

By then the fairground, which had developed from a ramshackle collection of stalls and coconut shies on the sands, was holding its own with neighbour Blackpool although there were still some who winced every time they heard the screams coming from the Helter Skelter Lighthouse and Maxim's Captive Flying Machine.

For Southport's more conservative residents, Pleasureland sat at odds with the resort's gentrified past, one built on the wealth of Victorian industrialists who had invested their fortunes in grand villas. On those same tree-lined avenues had

Previous pages: Away from Pleasureland, the beach provided a full programme of entertainment including this Punch and Judy show from the summer of 1950.

Left: Built by Victorian industrialists, Southport possessed tree-lined avenues, opulent hotels and some of the best shopping in the area.

Right: Despite significant opposition, Pleasureland opened in 1922 boasting rides like the Water Chute, Spinning Whip and River Caves.

sprung opulent hotels like the Royal Clifton and Birkdale Palace, and the wide expanse of Lord Street boasted some of the best shops in the whole of the North West.

The most well-heeled had considered a fairground far too down-market for Southport, but when fishermen and shrimpers began branching out into seaside entertainment the town planners, who had spent decades creating a meticulously ordered seafront, had no choice but to act. Holidaymakers, even the nice middle class ones favoured by the resort, were now demanding more than the odd donkey ride and the men in suits weren't going to be dictated to by a group of trawlermen.

'Seaside amusements date back to the late 1800s,' says Nick Laister. He works as a planning consultant to modern-day theme parks, but he's also blessed with an encyclopedic knowledge of the history of British thrill-seeking. 'But the fairgrounds and Pleasure Beaches as we know them today really took off between 1910 and 1920. These days we tend to think of theme parks as being for children, but back then they were firmly marketed at adults. Yes, it probably did change the atmosphere of the place, but there was no real option when even the smallest resorts along the coast were opening fairgrounds.

'Any town aspiring to be a major resort had to have a fairground. It was what the public wanted. It was as simple as that.'

With the rides moved away from the promenade, the new fairground, originally known as White City, enjoyed brief success before Southport, like so many other seaside resorts, effectively closed to tourists during the First World War. It was a chastening time economically and when the resort's guesthouses and hotels were once again open for business the mood had softened. To survive, Southport had to invest in rides guaranteed to deliver a white-knuckle thrill.

Thus Pleasureland was born, opening to the public in Easter 1922. The rather serious-sounding Parks and Foreshore Committee was responsible for the look of the place, insisting every stall adopted a uniform white and green colour scheme. The mayor and the rest of the civic party, who were among the first to try out the rides, looked a little sombre as, two-by-two, they boarded the Spinning Whip. For those dressed in three-piece suits and wearing chains of office, the rather more gentle River Caves seemed much more to their taste, but once the formalities were over, Pleasureland really came into its own.

Holidaymakers were content to spend hours and a significant amount of their cash at the ice cream stalls, the What the Butler Saw penny slot machines, and those who collected the coins from the electronic palm readers were rarely disappointed.

Above: Once inside, there was much to spend money on from ice cream stalls to penny slot machines and palm readers.

Opposite: At first, visitors were content to ride the big wheel and the waltzers, but by the late 1930s there was demand for a major roller coaster.

Whatever the reservations in more traditional quarters, Pleasureland was a success.

Holidaymakers were content to spend hours and a significant amount of their cash at the ice cream stalls, the What the Butler Saw penny slot machines, and those who collected the coins from the electronic palm readers were rarely disappointed.

Soon, alongside the mile-long Scenic Railway, Pleasureland had its own Ghost Train and Autodrome Electric Speedway, but it wasn't enough. It needed a grand statement. It got it in 1937 thanks to Charles Paige, an American engineer, who, two years earlier, had completed the Grand National, the giant wooden roller coaster at Blackpool's Pleasure Beach. Paige was highly regarded and his designs for the Cyclone didn't disappoint. From afar, it looked as if it had been constructed from thousands upon thousands of matchsticks, and the sound of the metal chain as it pulled the cars to the top of the slope was enough to set hearts racing.

'You've got to remember that no one drove fast cars and the pace of life was generally pretty slow,' says Nick. 'Suddenly these great wooden roller coasters were able to give people an adrenalin rush of the kind they had never had before. In Southport, you wouldn't have been able to miss the Cyclone; it was visible from every corner of the town. Every big fairground needs a flagship ride. It needs something to get people talking and the Cyclone certainly did that.'

Paige chose Joseph Emberton to design the entrance to the ride. Emberton was a forward-thinking architect who had already embraced the modernist style which had divided the public and critics alike. Many disliked the stark design, but Emberton was unapologetic. His belief was that with new methods of building at his disposal there was no justification for aping the styles of past generations. His contribution to Pleasureland may have been small, but the concrete tower with Cyclone in large letters down the side was unmissable.

The crowds returned and by the end of the decade it felt like it had never been more popular. Those halcyon, candy floss-tinted days continued through the 1950s and the 1960s.

The ride's very first passengers took their seats on Good Friday 1937. Each handed over sixpence and held on tight. Carrying eighteen people at a time, the carriages rose to 60ft, reached speeds of 42mph and their screams could be heard at the other end of the park.

So successful was Pleasureland's new attraction that it aroused the interest of the Thompson family. They had already turned Blackpool Pleasure Beach into the resort's major attraction and now began negotiations with Southport. However, the takeover plans were stalled by the outbreak of the Second World War. In December 1940, a letter landed on the desk of the town clerk. It was from the Air Ministry and simply said that Pleasureland was being requisitioned. The vast 14-acre site was perfect for storing aeroplanes, and anything in their way, including the Water Chute, was taken down.

Like a secondhand car, carefully maintained and run regularly, fairground rides can last for decades. Exposed to rain, wind and frost they quickly deteriorate. With Pleasureland declared a military site, the operators of the Cyclone, the Ferris Wheel and the Octopus were barred from entering, but they knew that behind the hoardings their livelihoods were eroding.

When the gates reopened, Pleasureland had seen much better days. It took weeks to remove the sand from the Cyclone's tracks and carriages and the owner of the Mountain Caterpillar returned to find an empty space where his ride had once been. Like the Water Chute, it had also been dismantled to make way for a new delivery of aircraft parts. Yet the crowds did return to Pleasureland and by the end of the decade it felt like it had never been more popular. Those candy floss-tinted days continued through the 1950s and the 1960s. Even when those

This page: Before concerns about environmental impact and congestion, holidaymakers with cars, such as these in 1959, would simply pull up onto the sand to pitch their spot.

Left: For Southport's teenage boys, Pleasureland proved the perfect place to meet girls and provided the backdrop for many a holiday romance.

Opposite: For those not tall enough to ride the Cyclone, there was always the opportunity for a spot of fishing.

who had traditionally spent a week in Southport came just for a day or two instead, Pleasureland was where they headed, and if they were running out of time they'd sacrifice most other things for a ride on the Cyclone.

By the 1980s, more than forty years after negotiations had first begun, the Thompson family finally took over Pleasureland. Their name and their experience held a lot of cachet and many assumed the long-term future of the site was secure. And so it was, right up until 5 September 2006 when an official statement was released by the directors: Pleasureland was to close. The decision was blamed in part on increased competition from publicly and Lottery-funded attractions and the official press release also noted that the relaxation of Sunday trading laws and a rise in the number of sporting events taking place on Sundays had damaged footfall.

Within a few paragraphs, it was all over. Or at least it was over, bar one final protest.

A fortnight after Pleasureland closed, and fearing that it was only a matter of time before the Cyclone was headed for the skip, two local residents, Peter Crompton and Alastair Bone, decided to launch a very visible protest. Under the banner of the Southport Preservation Society, the pair, who hoped to get the structure listed, decided to chain themselves to the top of the ride.

'It was part of Southport's heritage, it was a classic,' said Peter after he had agreed to end the

protest when police informed him the stunt was a dangerous distraction for the drivers of passing cars. 'It should never have been lost. You never get it back. Southport was built on tourism and grew on tourism and the roller coaster was an essential part of that. It was a welcome sign as you came from Preston and Liverpool – you knew you'd arrived. It was unbelievable that anyone would take it down. It was a last resort to go up there and we got some proper chains and padlocks so we couldn't be removed. In the eyes of the public what we did wasn't a crime, it was a public service.'

All attempts to get the ride listed proved unsuccessful. Less than two months after Peter and Alastair's protest, the Cyclone, which a few years earlier had been voted the number one wooden roller coaster by a member of the National Amusement Park Historical Association of America, was unceremoniously demolished.

'It all happened so quickly, but part of the wider problem was that English Heritage had never carried out a national survey of fairground rides,' says Nick, who in 2001 successfully petitioned to make the Scenic Railway in Margate's Dreamland the first fairground ride ever to be listed. 'The organisation has done a lot of work on churches, on cinemas and industrial buildings at risk, but I guess they felt seaside attractions didn't fit its brief.'

By the time Pleasureland closed, Nick had already set up the Dreamland Trust with the aim of

Opposite: Despite being built in 1937, the Cyclone stood the test of time and it remained Southport's most visible landmark until 2006.

Right: When the Thompson family took over Pleasureland in the 1980s, the park's future seemed assured.

'Britain's seaside resorts were built by entrepreneurs, not by councils. It took men of vision to come to the coast and take a risk. These were people who instinctively knew what the public wanted.'

reopening the Margate attraction as the country's first ever heritage theme park and he managed to salvage around ten of Southport's rides, including the Ghost Train, Fun House and River Caves. It was too late, though, to save the Cyclone. By the time English Heritage sent its experts to view the ride, it had already been partly demolished.

'There was no way back,' says Norman Wallis, who was one of the first on the site after the Thompson family left. His great-great-grandfather had opened a carousel in Southport at the turn of the twentieth century and his family's life has been intertwined with fairgrounds for more than 150 years. By the time Pleasureland closed he had worked as a theme parks consultant in Canada, Abu Dhabi and Kazakhstan, yet he was drawn back to the North West of England.

'The only word to describe what we found when we got on site was a shambles. It's easy to romanticise about the old wooden roller coasters, but they needed a lot of maintenance. I love the idea of preserving our heritage, but these places are businesses and to survive you have to be practical. When it comes to fairgrounds you have to keep moving forward and giving people bigger and better rides. People vote with their feet, that's just the way it is.'

Norman reopened the park the following summer. Now known as Southport Pleasureland, none of the old rides remain. Instead of the old Water Chute there's the Piranha River Ride, while the OMG and Transformer are now responsible for the screams. But Norman hopes one thing has remained the same.

'Britain's seaside resorts were built by entrepreneurs, not by councils. It took men of vision to come to the coast and take a risk. These were people who instinctively knew what the public wanted. In the 1930s that led to the Cyclone being built and I like to think that I'm just another link in the chain.'

W H I T L

EY BAY

There are various signs attached to buildings in Whitley Bay. Some are official, like the ones on various boarded-up guesthouses which read, 'Acquired by North Tyneside Council for redevelopment'. Others show a more creative spirit. At the end of a row of houses where the final seafront terrace was demolished some years ago, someone has painted a picture of waves over the rather sorry red-brick wall. On top is daubed the advice: 'You're looking the wrong way'.

It has been there so long that most of the residents don't give it a second look. However, if there is one sign still guaranteed to cause a reaction in this North East seaside town it's the one on the side of Spanish City. It reads simply: 'Ready to put the heart back into Whitley Bay.'

The slogan was first used in 2011 when the developer Robertson unveiled its grand plans to transform the building which had already lain empty for years. Back then, the proposals included a fifty-bed four-star hotel, skate park, cinema and café offering views along the coast to St Mary's lighthouse, but three years on the hoardings are still up and Spanish City is still awaiting restoration.

'Think of a use for Spanish City and I'll guarantee someone else will have been there before,' says Charlie Steel just as we round the corner and the iconic dome comes into view. 'They've talked about turning it into an arts centre, they've suggested it could be a hotel. At various points it looked certain it was going to be flats and at one stage it was even mooted that it could become a school.

'I think that's part of the problem. Everyone would love to wind back the clock and have a thriving entertainment complex here, but I just don't think it would be sustainable, so then what do you do? If you don't have a vision, you just end up doing nothing. They say they are ready to put the heart back into Whitley Bay, but a lot of people round here will tell you that the heart of this place was ripped out the day Spanish City closed.'

Charlie, who grew up just down the road in Monkseaton, worked for the police force for more than thirty years and, now semi-retired, he has been able to devote more time to researching the area's history.

'It doesn't look good, does it?' he says, pointing to the roof, where a large patch has turned an unappealing shade of brown. 'They painted it a couple of years ago, but now it's covered in moss. Everyone hopes that it will be restored, but the plans have stalled so many times that people have got used to disappointment.'

Even in its redundant state, Spanish City looms large over the small resort just as it did when it first opened in 1910. It was the brainchild of Charles

Previous pages: In July, 1953, a mini-heatwave saw 20,000 people pack the beach at Whitley Bay, although some of the men refused to remove their suit jackets.

Left: The Virginia Reel was one of the first rides to arrive at Spanish City, which opened to the public in 1910.

WATER CHUTE SPANISH CITY WHITLEY BAY

The striking white turrets and latticed windows were Moorish in style and the central dome ensured it stood apart from every other seaside entertainment complex.

EMPRESS BALLROOM, WHITLEY BAY.

Above: Spanish City was built by entertainer and businessman Charles Elderton, who recognised the resort's need for a large venue.

Left: In the Empress Ballroom, which replaced the original theatre, up to a thousand couples could take to the floor each night.

WHITLEY B

IT'S QUICKER BY RAIL

NEW GUIDE FREE FROM L·N·E·R OFFICES AND AGENCIES OR COUNCI

Published by the LONDON & NORTH EASTERN RAILWAY

OFFICES, WHITLEY BAY

JARROLD & SONS LTD. NORWICH & LONDON

Elderton of the Theatre Royal in Hebburn who had been bringing his Toreadors Concert Party to the town for a number of summers. Like many of the early Pierrot troupes, they performed outdoors with only a canvas awning, in their case painted with scenes of Spain, for protection. However, as audience numbers increased, Elderton grew keen on establishing a permanent venue in the emerging resort.

Until a few years earlier Whitley, as it was then known, had been little more than a fishing village, but the first step in its rebranding as a seaside destination had occurred following a slightly unfortunate mix-up with a corpse. In 1897, a man – his name is not given in any of the reports from the time – died some way from his beloved Whitley. Keen to fulfil his last wish to be buried at the coast, his coffin was put on a train and at Whitley station undertakers waited to take him on his final journey. Except the coffin never arrived. Enquiries revealed

Above: The dodgems, photographed here in 1950, were one of the most popular rides in the fairground.

Left: In the 1920s, Whitley Bay launched a major publicity drive with London and North Eastern Railway to promote the resort to southern holidaymakers.

it had been sent to Whitby and the funeral had to be postponed until the next day. The post office was already weary with the quantity of mail that had to be redirected to and from the Yorkshire town, but having a dead man turn up there was the final straw. A change of name was needed and so plain old Whitley became Whitley Bay.

The addition of those three little letters helped market the area to holidaymakers and, around the same time as work was beginning on Spanish City, Joseph Lawson was starting his own seaside enterprise, hiring out deckchairs on the beach. Nearby, the fairground with its water chute, and figure of eight railway was already doing brisk business, but Elderton's ambitious building would be the resort's crowning glory. The striking white turrets and latticed windows were Moorish in style and the central dome ensured it stood apart from every other seaside entertainment complex. Second only to St Paul's Cathedral in size, it changed the skyline of this small corner of the North East for ever.

Inside was a spacious theatre with room for 1,400 in the main auditorium and a further 400 in the gallery and, with the roof garden, various souvenir shops and cafés, it was designed to ensure that once inside, no one left until their purses or wallets were empty.

Below left: Some prefer to relax standing up, like this man photographed on the sands in 1958.

Below: In its 1950s heyday the sands of Whitley Bay were packed with holidaymakers and during August most guesthouses were fully booked.

By 1954, the council had taken over Joe Lawson's business. Its stock had risen to 5,500 deckchairs, 300 tents and 50 windbreakers and Whitley Bay was widely referred to as both the 'Playground of the North' and the 'North East's answer to Blackpool'. At Spanish City, business boomed.

The town's motto is *Non Sibi Sed Omnibus* (Not For Oneself But For all) and with Spanish City proving popular with holidaymakers from the North East, Whitley Bay's tourism chiefs decided that they needed to spread the word much further afield. In 1925 a major publicity campaign was launched. With the London and North Eastern Railway agreeing to pick up a third of the bill, advertisements appeared in national newspapers, billboards were printed and the first ever Whitley Bay holiday guide was launched. While modern brochures rely on beautiful photography and persuasive editorial, back then things tended to be more direct.

'The air of the district is dry and bracing and the breezes of the mountain air from the Northumbrian Hills have a revitalising and invigorating effect,' ran one editorial, before helpfully adding: 'The death rate is the lowest in Northumberland.'

It might not have been subtle, but it did the trick. By 1954, the council had taken over Joe Lawson's business. Its stock had risen to 5,500 deckchairs, 300 tents and 50 windbreakers and Whitley Bay was being widely referred to as both the 'Playground of the North' and the 'North East's answer to Blackpool'. At Spanish City business boomed.

Palm readers and phrenologists, who claimed to tell the future by reading the bumps of the skull, had set up stalls in the fairground, and in the Empress Ballroom, which had replaced the original theatre some years earlier, up to a thousand couples regularly danced the night away to the tunes of bandleaders like Jos Q Atkinson and Billy Ternent.

'It was an adventure playground right on my doorstep,' says Stanley Graham, whose parents ran the pub at the Corner House Hotel. 'During Glasgow fortnight in early August families flooded down the north east coast, filling up the boarding houses and, of course, Spanish City. I used to collect them from the railway station, load their cases on my barrow and walk them down to where they were staying. It was a great little earner and funded many a night out. From our house, looking out over the rooftops, I could see the reflection of the coloured lights and hear the rumble of the Figure of Eight roller coaster.

'Close to the brightly painted carousel was one of my favourite stalls, the Grand National horse racing game. You rolled a ball up a slope and the horse would move a certain number of places depending

This page: By the 1950s, Whitley Bay had established itself as a genuine rival to Blackpool and was billing itself as the Playground of the North.

which hole it went in. The secret was the attendant could push down on the mechanism behind the rolling area and give any horses a winning gallop. I was always careful to play when someone I knew was running the stall and consequently won quite a few races, miraculously coming from behind with an amazing last-minute spurt.'

Spanish City's Picture House cinema with its Axminster carpet, oak-panelled walls, plush seating and ornamental plasterwork was visible evidence of the money starting to pour into Whitley Bay and no one had any reason to suspect the situation would change.

'When I was young, on a weekend everyone would head to Spanish City, including the locals,' says Charlie. 'It was a regular haunt for everyone round here. If you asked most people where they were going to be on Saturday night, they'd tell you they were going to be down the Spanner. We thought it would be there forever.'

Even a reporter from *The Times*, who in 1969 was sent out to do a round-up of Britain's best holidays, was forced to admit that Whitley Bay was still an attractive resort.

'The North East is not usually the first corner of Britain to spring to mind when planning a holiday,' he began, in a nod to the northern clog-wearing stereotypes which still pervaded the national press. 'Those who have taken the trouble to find that the region is not all slag heaps, back-to-back houses and shipyards, that the temperature does frequently rise above freezing and that the smoke of industry is confined to a narrow strip have found that it offers some of the most rewarding holidays in Britain.'

For Shaun Prendergast, who grew up in the resort during the 1970s, Spanish City promised more than that. It promised girls.

'On Bank Holidays the place was awash with hormones as hordes of kids descended on the place

and wandered round the stalls jingling the pitiful change in their pockets. We had one eye on the girls, but the other warily watched the competition. There were natty guys, blokes in suits, but the undisputed kings of the fair were the waltzer lads. One could roll a cigarette one-handed like a cowboy and he danced between the cars with it permanently clenched between his teeth. A constant single tear tracked down his cheek from his smoke-filled inflamed eye, but he still used it to wink at the girls and it worked.'

For Shaun there was no better place to be, but not everyone agreed. While the bingo hall now occupying the old Empress Ballroom continued to pack them in, the rest of the site gradually fell into decline. A sharp drop in the number of families holidaying in the resort meant there was no one to frequent the venue's shops and cafés and even the addition of the 60mph Corkscrew roller coaster in the early 1980s provided only a temporary lifeline. The fairground's demolition was announced in December 1999. Three years later, the last of the amusement operators left and North Tyneside Council, which now owned the buildings, was left wondering what to do with this giant ghost of seaside past.

'It was in a pretty bad state,' says Mick Sharp, a local designer, who a few years ago staged an exhibition to mark Spanish City's centenary back inside the famous dome. 'Before any use could be found for the building it needed a lot of painstaking restoration work and it was unfortunate that when it was completed the country went into recession. We should be thankful that it hasn't been demolished like a lot of these old seaside buildings, but having it stood empty all these years hasn't been good for the area.'

Back on the seafront, a two-day food and drink festival is under way. Among the stallholders is Luciano di Meo. It was his great-great-grandfather Isidoro who started the family's ice cream business, walking from southern Italy to find his fortune in the North East, and the secret family recipe has been passed down through the generations.

'We've not had anything like this for years,' says Luciano, who runs an ice cream parlour just a short stroll from the sands. 'Isidoro began selling ice cream from a barrow and it's testament to everyone's hard work that we are still here a century on. I remember my grandfather teaching me how to make ice cream when I was just a boy of eight years old. It's in my blood and there was nothing I would rather be doing. You can't have a seaside resort without ice cream.'

The rain holds off and by the end of the afternoon most of the traders are leaving with empty stalls and full cash boxes. The time when Glasgow's factory workers stayed in Whitley Bay for a week or two might be gone, but as the sun sets on another summer's day it seems Whitley Bay might finally have a future worth celebrating.

Opposite: The dome of the Spanish City was second only in size to St Paul's Cathedral and was visible for miles around.

Right: The construction of the iconic Corkscrew roller coaster in the 1980s symbolised a new chapter for Spanish City, but sadly it didn't last long.

NEW BR

IGHTON

Recently a new attraction arrived on the beach at New Brighton. The brainchild of local artist Frank Lund, it's called the *Black Pearl* and there's no way to describe it other than a pirate ship fashioned from driftwood.

In part, it's a nod to the past. Up until the nineteenth century the area was a hotbed of smuggling and, while no one seems to be able to pinpoint an exact location, secret underground tunnels are still rumoured to exist in the area. The *Black Pearl* is also carrying on another New Brighton tradition, that of resilient ambition. In its first twelve months, the ship was both destroyed by fire and washed away in a storm, yet Frank and his army of volunteers rebuilt it and, should disaster strike a third time, they'll no doubt do so again.

That same enterprising spirit was in evidence 180 years earlier when wealthy merchant James Atherton crossed the River Mersey and stood for the first time on Rock Point. Buying 170 acres of undeveloped heathland and sand hills, the Cheshire-born grocer had a plan. On this barren stretch of land he would build a resort where Liverpool's gentry, growing rich on the sugar, spice and cotton passing through the city's docks, could relax. His blueprint would be Brighton on the south coast and his version would have everything the existing resort possessed – only it would be bigger and better.

Atherton died just six years into the project, but by then others had realised the potential of a resort with a fine beach and views across the Irish Sea. Streets of grand villas began to take shape and when the renowned architect Eugenius Birch agreed to design a new pier to replace the rather ramshackle affair erected to give labourers access to the site, the resort had arrived. By the late 1860s, New Brighton was luring tourists, dressed in their Sunday best, with the promise of fine sands, a grand promenade and fresh sea air.

Over the next fifty years it would boast a tower bigger than Blackpool's and an outdoor bathing pool and theatre which both claimed to be the largest of their kind in the world. From the other side of the Mersey, the twinkling lights of New Brighton seemed like another world.

'New Brighton had everything, it really did,' says Paul Halliday, manager of the Floral Pavilion, just one of seven theatres to survive from the resort's heyday. 'People coming here for the first time find that hard to believe. Yes, they think it must be a nice place to live, but they don't realise that there was a time when New Brighton was known to everyone on Merseyside and beyond as one of the best resorts in the North West.'

Rewind, then, to the dawn of the twentieth century when, after four years and the death of six labourers, New Brighton's landmark tower was

NEW BRIGHTON, THE TOWER
AND THE SANDS 1900 45163

Left: New Brighton had every attraction to match its namesake resort on the south coast. Here visitors are photographed in the 1940s heading to the Tower Ballroom.

Below: For those who grew up in Liverpool, the lights of New Brighton represented a magical world of possibilities.

By the 1930s New Brighton had become a byword for fun and glamour and the open-air bathing pool was to be the jewel in its crown. South-facing, its walls were designed to act both as a suntrap and a windbreak and its record-breaking size allowed 12,000 to pack in for the official opening in 1934. By the end of that first week some 100,000 had paid to go through the turnstiles.

Previous pages: The pier was designed by the renowned architect Eugenius Birch and for many years boasted its own one-legged diver.

Opposite left: In the 1950s, the famous ferries across the River Mersey were carrying three million passengers a year.

Opposite far left: New Brighton's tower was bigger than Blackpool's, but it wouldn't prove to be quite so enduring as its rival.

just about to open. At 544ft, it eclipsed Blackpool Tower by 26ft and was the tallest and, according to its champions, the most elegant structure in the country. Four lifts carried passengers to the viewing platform where on a clear day you could see the Isle of Man, Great Orme and the Welsh mountains. Yet its rival would prove more enduring. Lack of maintenance during the First World War did for the tower and, having been declared unsafe in 1919, the 1,000 tonnes of steel came down rather more quickly than they had gone up. While the fate of the iconic structure was an embarrassment for the local dignitaries who had snapped up the £1 shares, its demise failed to dent New Brighton's growing popularity.

Most visitors arrived by ferry, climbing aboard the *Royal Iris* and the *Royal Daffodil* at Liverpool dockside for the short journey across the water. There to greet them most days was 'Peggy' Gadsby, who had been heading for a successful career as a footballer with Notts County until he lost a leg while serving with the Sherwood Foresters in 1918. What brought him to New Brighton in the 1920s no one is quite sure, but having discovered he could still swim with one leg he spotted a gap in the market.

Using the pier as his diving board, Gadsby would time his spectacular tumbles to coincide with the arrival of ferries. On special occasions he would swap his black tights and woollen bathing cap for a red and white striped costume and, as the passengers disembarked, he would be standing there, fishing net in hand, to collect the pennies.

Gadsby's aquatic acrobatics, which spanned more than forty years, were just the start of New Brighton's attractions. There was the roller skating rink, the monkey house and aviary and the cycle track where, in 1922, the World Championships were held. Most visitors, though, came for the dances in the Tower Ballroom where as many as 1,000 couples would take to the floor as the sixty-strong orchestra played through the night. Painted white and gold, its decor incorporating various emblems of Lancashire towns, the venue was the backdrop for a thousand romances and provided the spark for numerous brief encounters as single men headed for the balcony to spot a potential partner among the dancers below.

Once they were tired of dancing, couples would stroll through the 35 acres of gardens where brass bands played, tightrope walkers performed on high wires and gondoliers sang in Italian as they rowed across the large lake. New Brighton didn't buy into the idea that small is beautiful.

Every development was on a grand scale. The stage of the Tower Theatre alone was 45ft wide, the auditorium could hold 3,500, and the programme was equally ambitious. One summer a Wild West Show was booked from America for a six-month season. Highland cattle were brought down from Scotland for the cowboys to lasso, but there were also reports that the troupe had a tendency to demonstrate their roping talents on New Brighton's unsuspecting female population.

By the 1930s New Brighton had become a byword for fun and glamour and the open-air bathing pool was to be the jewel in its crown. South-facing, its walls were designed to act both as a suntrap and a windbreak and its record-breaking size allowed 12,000 to pack in for the official opening in 1934. By the end of that first week some 100,000 had paid to go through the turnstiles.

Fifteen years later it was also the scene of the very first Miss New Brighton beauty contest. While the first heat attracted only nine entrants, by the time of the final, when Edna McFarlane collected her cup and a cheque for £75 in front of 15,000 spectators, the beauty pageant, already a staple at resorts like Morecambe, had come of age in New Brighton. For many girls from working-class families like Lillian Jones, the competitions seemed impossibly glamorous.

'I remember my cousin dared me to enter. We weren't terribly well-off and she said if I did, she would give me a pair of her shoes. I can remember them now, crocodile skin they were, strappy and with the highest of heels. Daily life back then was pretty humdrum and this was a distraction, a little escape.

'There were some of the girls who treated pageants like a full-time job, but I always viewed it as just a fun day out. I made my own dress, did my own

Opposite: Sisters, Susan and Hazel McKinley, from the Wirral, were photographed devouring candyfloss on New Brigthon's promenade in April 1959.

They were there for Operation Big Beat and each had paid five shillings and sixpence to hear Gerry and the Pacemakers, Kingsize Taylor and the Dominoes, Rory Storm and the Hurricanes and the Remo Four. The headline act that night was a relatively unknown Liverpudlian band. They were called The Beatles.

hair and make-up. I couldn't believe it when I won, so I thought I might as well have a go at a few more.'

Which was how in 1950 she came to be standing on the edge of the New Brighton pool in a bright white swimming costume. By then Lillian was married and, while a few years older than some of the other girls, she was named runner-up to Violet Pretty, who would become known to many a few years later as the Hollywood actress Anne Heywood. In 1967 Heywood would star in *The Fox* which featured a controversial lesbian scene, but back then Lillian remembers her as a shy young thing.

'The competition was held during the day and that evening they took over a cinema for the formal presentations. Violet was only seventeen and she was terrified. I remember her sat in between me and my husband. We were both holding her hands and you could feel her shaking. For those who saw it as a springboard into show business there was a lot of pressure on how well you did.'

The competition would continue until 1989, but as the years ticked by, behind the fixed smiles and perfectly set hair was a resort struggling to keep up with the times. Some said New Brighton had never really been the same after the Second World War, while others blamed the Betting and Gambling Act for hammering the final nails in the coffin. After the Act became law on 1 May 1961, betting shops began opening at the rate of a hundred a week and bingo hit the British seaside like a tidal wave. As developers looked to turn every available hall, cinema and theatre into a bingo hall, in New Brighton there were reports of mothers sending their children to save their place in the queue while they cleared up after dinner.

Many traditional attractions began to look old-fashioned, yet there was one corner of the resort where modern tastes were still being satisfied. On 10 November 1961, the Tower Ballroom was once again packed. This time the crowd was not

Left: In August 1964, The Rolling Stones added their name to the list of famous acts to play the Tower Ballroom.

Opposite: The Beatles appeared at the venue twenty-seven times, giving their final performance on 14 June 1963.

NEMS ENTERPRISES PRESENT AT

NEW BRIGHTON TOWER
FOR ONE NIGHT ONLY 7.30 to 11.30
FRIDAY, JUNE 14th.

Merseyside's Greatest...

THE BEATLES
AND
GERRY and the PACEMAKERS

TICKETS

6/- IN ADVANCE ✳ AT DOOR ON NIGHT **7/-**

A BOB WOOLER PRODUCTION

PLUS 5 GREAT SUPPORTING GROUPS!!

DON'T MISS

FRIDAY, JUNE 28th.
JET HARRIS & TONY MEEHAN

Right: The resort's open-air swimming pool provided the backdrop for the annual Miss New Brighton competition.

Below: Violet Pretty, later better-known as the Hollywood actress Anne Heywood, was one of the early winners of the New Brighton beauty contest.

Violet was only seventeen and she was terrified. I remember her sat in between me and my husband. We were both holding her hands and you could feel her shaking. For those who saw it as a springboard into show business there was a lot of pressure on how well you did.'

interested in dancing, at least not the kind that required any formal lessons.

They were there for Operation Big Beat and each had paid five shillings and sixpence to hear Gerry and the Pacemakers, Kingsize Taylor and the Dominoes, Rory Storm and the Hurricanes and the Remo Four. The headline act that night was a relatively unknown Liverpudlian band. They were called The Beatles.

'New Brighton has always been special to me,' says Sam Leach, who was the driving force behind Operation Big Beat. 'I'll never forget that surge of excitement as a child when the bus came over the rise by Liverpool Town Hall and we descended towards the ferries. Once on board we knew that there was just fifteen minutes between us and the fairground, the fish and chips and the beach.

'When I was older, New Brighton was where I used to go dancing on Saturday nights. There was just something special about the Tower and to me it seemed the perfect venue for a concert.'

Sam had approached the Tower execs, Tom McCardle and Bill Roberts, about his plan in the October. They were doubtful it would be quite the success he hoped but with the Tower having become something of a white elephant they agreed to give him a go.

'I remember asking what the previous record attendance had been and they roared with laughter. They told me I had no chance of beating the 3,300 who a good few years earlier had watched the Joe Loss Orchestra, one of the most successful acts of the big band era. They were still laughing as I let myself out.'

Sam planned Operation Big Beat like a military operation. Ticket agents were contacted, large advertisements were placed in the local newspaper and a series of special late-night buses were put on to ensure the concertgoers could get home after the show.

'When I returned to the Tower with the posters and flyers, Tom leapt up and shouted excitedly: "Sam, the phone hasn't stopped with people wanting tickets – we said it would be fantastic, didn't we, Bill?" I had to laugh, but thanked them for their support.'

Operation Big Beat drew a 4,100-strong crowd and when the show was repeated two weeks later 4,600 passed through the doors of the Tower Ballroom.

'All the kids were screaming and crying. I still shiver when I recall the atmosphere because it was so

electric. They never played to a bigger crowd in Britain and while it's a gig rarely mentioned, for me and many others that was the night Beatlemania was born.'

Sam admits that he was a rock 'n' roll fan masquerading as a promoter and after a year or so of organising Friday night concerts at the Tower, he gave it up. By then he had a young family and, while he might have been persuaded to return, in 1969 a fire swept through the Tower Ballroom. By the time firemen arrived the only thing worth rescuing was a stash of toys destined to be prizes for the fairground stalls. The place was gutted and, while the decision not to rebuild was met with opposition, financially it just didn't make sense.

In 1955, the New Brighton ferries had carried three million passengers. By 1970, the service was only operating in the summer months and numbers had dropped to below 300,000. The oldest and cheapest route between Wallasey and Liverpool had reached crisis point. The last boat sailed on 26 September 1971, and New Brighton's days as a major resort were numbered.

Six years later the pier was demolished and, while the open-air pool survived until 1990, by the time part of the structure collapsed following a heavy storm, it had already seen better days.

Today New Brighton is largely residential. There's no tower, no grand ballroom and no vast open-air pool. In fact, the only nod to its past is a small blue plaque which remembers the time The Beatles came to town.

Right: With the arrival of rock 'n' roll, the Tower Ballroom began to cater for a different audience, one which couldn't and didn't want to waltz or foxtrot.

LLAND

UDNO

There's a plot of land just at the bottom of Great Orme, the rocky outcrop which looms large over Llandudno, which should now be home to a Covent Garden-style market. It should be bustling with visitors heading for the new exhibition space and cafés which were supposed to give the grand Pier Pavilion a secure future.

There are still many in the town, long ago dubbed the Queen of Welsh resorts, who still hanker after what might have been. Its owners were about to put the scheme out to tender in 1994 when a fire, the kind responsible for the destruction of so much seaside heritage, ripped through the place. Within a few hours all that remained of more than a hundred years of history and those ambitious plans for the future were ashes and twisted metal.

The only thing to be grateful for was that Alex Munro was no longer around to see another of his beloved theatres come to such a sad end. Munro was one of the last of the great showmen, an entertainer who was never knowingly off-duty. For more than thirty years he was Mr Llandudno and his daughter, Anna-Marie, soon learnt she would have to share her father with the rest of the resort.

'Whenever I talk about the Llandudno I knew growing up, it feels like a completely different world,' she says. 'If we needed to get anywhere quickly it was a nightmare being with Dad. Every few yards he would be stopped by someone wanting to have a chat. Often it was holidaymakers who had seen one of his shows. Dad didn't know them, but they felt like they knew him. That was why he was so successful, he was everyone's best friend.'

Munro was born in Scotland on 6 March 1911, and along with his brother, Archie, and sister, June, he had formed an acrobatic troupe, joining Florrie Forde's Music Hall Company. Destined for the stage from an early age, he spent the Second World War entertaining troops in the RAF and afterwards returned to the music-hall circuit where his name gradually crept up the bill. Munro was an all-rounder. He might not have been the best singer or dancer in the world, but he knew how to work a crowd and when he eventually settled in Llandudno during the 1950s he soon became a familiar face to holidaymakers. With his bow tie and trademark trilby, there was no mistaking the compère and comedian as he tripped down the promenade across to Happy Valley, an open-air theatre and his second home during the summer months for more than thirty years.

'It was basically a natural amphitheatre and the facilities were pretty basic,' says Anna-Marie. 'There was somewhere for the company to change and a place selling ice creams, but that was about it.

Previous pages: The *Mirror* newspaper used to provide seaside entertainment. Here, in 1937 The Mirror 8 acrobatic display team performed for the crowds.

Left: Street performers are not a new phenomena. As far back as 1934, a robot was turning heads on Llandudno's promenade.

Left: The resort's open-air theatre, Happy Valley, was run by Alex Munro who would arrange lifts to the top of the steep hill for less able guests.

Below: Alwen Griffiths photographed as a young child, strolling along the Llandudno pier with her father. Many years later she would work at the Pier Pavilion as an usherette.

'As well as his own acts, Dad also ran talent shows. They were incredibly popular. It gave people an outlet to perform and I'll always remember one man who spent his entire week's holiday doing his Al Jolson impersonation.

'The audience would sit on deckchairs watching the singers, dancers, magicians and comedians and people often referred to it as "If Wet Townhall" because that's the sign we'd put up in case it rained. I'm sure there must have been downpours, but you know what? I honestly don't remember many at all, even the summers seemed better back then.'

With only staff cars allowed to drive up the hill to Happy Valley, Munro would ferry the oldest and more infirm audience members to and from the venue and he also showed an enlightened attitude to those who tried to evade the box office.

'There's a hill nearby overlooking Happy Valley and it would be packed with people who wanted

Left: Alex Munro pictured with his daughter, the actress Janet Munro, two years before her sudden death in 1972 at the age of 38.

Right: The Pier Pavilion started off as a classical concert venue, but as tastes changed the programme gave way to more popular acts.

Munro was one of the last of the great showmen, an entertainer who was never knowingly off duty. For more than thirty years he was Mr Llandudno and his daughter, Anna-Marie, soon learnt she would have to share her father with the rest of the resort.

to see the show, but who didn't want to pay for a ticket,' remembers Anna-Marie. 'Dad didn't mind, he used to call it Aberdeen Hill. As a Scot himself, he reckoned he could get away with calling them miserly and I used to be sent up there to rattle a bottle in the hope they would be persuaded to make a small donation.'

After every lunchtime show, Munro would grab a lie-down in preparation for the evening when he would be back again, checking the acts were ready for their twice-nightly performance in one of Llandudno's other venues.

Munro was a man who lived and breathed variety shows. When he wasn't on the phone booking a new act, he could often be found up a ladder carrying out some urgent repair to the safety curtain or checking the numerous hoardings and bill posters, each featuring his photograph, which appeared around the town. By early evening, Munro was at his regular post outside the main entrance to the box office, greeting early arrivals and doing his best salesman pitch to those who happened to be passing by. Most

soon found themselves at the box office buying tickets for that night's performance.

Munro's *Startime* shows ran at the Pavilion from May to October for a number of seasons and regularly featured the likes of Billy Crockett, the mad musician from London, who played miniature harmonicas and a tiny saxophone. His nights promised 'melodious melodies, glamorous girls and clean comedy' and it was the continuation of a tradition which had begun with the official opening of the Pier Pavilion back in 1886.

Music had initially been the big sell with the sound of Rivère's Orchestra carried along on the sea breeze, but as tastes changed, by the mid-1930s concerts had given way to variety entertainment and the theatre was run by a succession of managers like Alex Munro.

Alwen Griffiths spent six years as one of the Pier Pavilion's twenty-two usherettes. During the day she worked as a receptionist and secretary at the *Llandudno Advertiser* Office and Printing Works where the programmes she would sell each night were produced.

PIER PAVILION

General Manager: T. TURNER PILLING   Tel. 76258

Llandudno

Week Commencing SEPTEMBER 10 ★ 6 NIGHTS AT 8 p.m.

ROBINSON CLEAVER presents

THE WYN CALVIN SHOW

A HAPPY REVUSICAL

Starring

The Welsh Prince of Laughter

WYN CALVIN

BETTINA RICHMAN
and JOHN JACKSON
The Bright and Breezy Two-some

GUEST CELEBRITY
Star of Stage, Screen
Radio and Television
JANET BROWN

SANDRA
and the BOY FRIENDS
'A Singing Gal –
4 Swinging Guys'

T.V.'s GLAMOROUS
KIM TRACEY
Singing and Swinging

"THE MELODY MAN"
George Hildrew

RADIO'S POPULAR
BOBBY PAGAN
HAMMOND ORGAN TRIO

! BALLET BODEGA !
12 MARIE DE VERE DANCERS 12

BOOK NOW! 7/6 6/6, 5/6, 4/6, 3/- (Reserved)   2/- Unreserved
Accompanied children 2/6 all parts
Box office open daily 10 a.m. to 6 p.m.   Phone 76258
Telephone bookings MUST be claimed by 7.45 p.m. on day of performance

PIER PAVILION
Llandudno

Telephone — 75259

General Manager — — — — — JOHN MILLS

SUNDAY, 15th JULY, 1979, at 8 p.m.

ROBINSON CLEAVER and CLIVE STOCK

present

★ **FIRST TIME HERE** ★

FRANKIE VAUGHAN

"Give Me the Moonlight"!

MAELGWN MALE VOICE CHOIR
60 — GLORIOUS VOICES OF WALES — 60

THE MINTING SISTERS
THREE HITS AND EACH ONE A MISS

ROBINSON CLEAVER
B.B.C. AND RECORDING STAR ORGANIST

SOUVENIR PROGRAMME

'We had to get to the theatre before the doors opened at 7.30p.m. so we could be issued with our programmes and later we'd go back to collect the ices to sell at the interval. At the end of the week we received commission on what we'd sold, although they kept some back until the end of the season to make sure we didn't leave halfway through.

'I remember the theatre was packed every night and we worked six nights a week, seating two thousand people in half an hour. One evening, two young men came in and one said to me, "Is it OK if I stand at the back?" I replied, "Yes, if you have a ticket". They smiled and when I looked closer I realised one was the star of the show, Max Bygraves, who wanted to check the sound at the back of the theatre. It was wonderful, really, I got to see so many stars like Petula Clark, then a young girl of seventeen, George Formby, Arthur Askey, the Beverley Sisters, Alma Cogan and the very popular Welsh singer Ivor Emmanuel.'

Known as the Voice of Wales, Emmanuel regularly topped the bill on Sunday evenings in Llandudno. He'd grown up in Pontrhydyfen, the same Welsh village as lifelong friend Richard Burton, but when his parents, sisters and grandfather were killed by a stray bomb during the Second World War, the future had looked bleak for young Ivor. Taken in by his aunt, it seemed he was destined for a life down the mines. However, whenever he had the chance he would carry his wind-up gramophone to the top of a nearby mountain. Far away from the soot and claustrophobia of the pits, he would turn up the volume as high as it would go and, listening to the recordings of the Italian tenor Enrico Caruso, dream of a better life. It was Burton who arranged for his old friend to audition for a part in a London production of the musical *Oklahoma!* Having been turned down countless times before, Emmanuel had doubted whether he would ever make it as a professional, but *Oklahoma!* would be his big break. Without it, he would never have been cast in the film *Zulu* as Private Owen, who leads the defenders of Rorke's Drift in a stirring rendition of the Welsh battle anthem 'Men of Harlech' and Sunday evenings at the Pier Pavilion in Llandudno would have been very different.

'Ah, yes, Ivor Emmanuel, or Ivor Enamel as I used to always call him, what a voice,' says comedian Wyn Calvin. Known as the Clown Prince of Wales, he was another regular on the bill. 'In many ways the Pier Pavilion was an odd little theatre. It was long and narrow and it felt a bit like performing in the Mersey Tunnel, but while it wasn't the grandest of the seaside theatres it did have a special atmosphere. You always felt very close to the audience. Llandudno was on the tour of every major act. Anyone who was anyone had played there and during those later summer seasons many were there because of Alex. He was the ultimate performer. As a Scotsman playing to largely English audiences in Wales, he had to be.'

While Munro always believed there was a place for family entertainment at the seaside, he also knew that the takings didn't lie. When the popularity of his *Startime* show first began to dip in the 1960s, he began to explore new ways of getting audiences through the doors. It was why in 1972 he announced the pavilion's first ever pantomime would be *Babes in the Wood* and it would star his eldest daughter. It was something of a coup for the town. Janet Munro had already made her name in Hollywood, having been signed to Walt Disney's studio where she starred in *The Swiss Family Robinson* and she had been one of Britain's rising stars. Her personal life had been turbulent, but after two divorces, treatment for alcoholism and a serious car crash, Janet was planning a comeback and a part in her father's first pantomime would mark her return. However, just days before rehearsals were due to begin, Janet suffered a fatal heart attack. She was just thirty-eight.

'I was only very young, but it was obviously a desperately sad time and Dad was quite inconsolable for a while,' says Anna-Marie, who was Janet's half-sister. 'As I grew up I knew I could never replace Janet, no one could, but I did feel that I somehow needed to step in and almost become a substitute "Daddy's girl".

'I was just two weeks old when Dad brought me on stage for the first time and I made my singing debut while I was still in primary school. Mum was a choreographer and dancer so if she was also involved in a show I'd often have to get a taxi home from school. I'd get out and then go straight to selling ice creams or raffle tickets. There was never a question of just sitting around, there were always jobs to do and you just got on and did it.'

Alex gave his life to the entertainment business, but not even his dedication could ensure the survival of variety in Llandudno.

Left: Ivor Emmanuel, known as the Voice of Wales, performed in summer seasons right up to the 1980s and was a regular on the bill at the Pier Pavilion.

'Dad never retired, I'm not sure he could have ever walked away. It was after the season ended in 1985 that he became ill. At first he was convinced it was just something he'd eaten, but it turned out it was cancer. He was riddled with it and he died three months later. I was nineteen years old and while variety entertainment was probably already on its way out, I'd always imagined I'd join the family business. However, without Dad there really was no business.'

The open-air theatre in Happy Valley closed and over the next decade, as Anna-Marie was working towards a Royal Academy of Music qualification which would see her remain in Llandudno as a singing teacher, the Pier Pavilion passed through the hands of various new owners. None seemed able to find a viable use for the place until it was bought by the Worcester-based company Launchsign Ltd.

There was much support for the plans to turn it into a covered market and, had Alex Munro been around on the evening of 13 February 1994 to do one last check for discarded cigarette ends, they might have come to fruition. Unfortunately he wasn't and by the time someone called 999 it was too late. As firemen and local councillors surveyed the scene the following morning, all knew that any opportunity to save the Pier Pavilion had been lost.

The site remains empty, although just a few minutes' walk away there is a reminder of the days when variety was king. Cars can now drive up to Happy Valley and, in April 2014, the road leading to the site of the former open-air theatre was renamed Alex Munro Way. It was a small tribute to the man who always suspected that Llandudno would never find anyone to replace him.

As he said in an interview to the *Sunday Times Magazine*: 'Don't you think it's a shame that when I am gone there'll be no one left doing my type of show? A simple man with a simple show. And, oh they love it . . . they love it to death.'

LEE-ON-TH

E-SOLENT

It was in the 1960s that Nikolaus Pevsner arrived in Hampshire, pen poised, to deliver another detailed and honest account of English architecture. His epic project to chronicle the country's buildings had begun in 1945 and would result in forty-six volumes. Among the many thousands of words he wrote about churches, theatres, town halls and libraries, in the Hampshire volume of his celebrated *Buildings of England* series, the German-born academic reserved just a few lines for the Lee Tower Complex.

'A good piece of second-rate inter-war modernism of the slightly jazzy sort, constructed of concrete when concrete seemed very to date,' he began, before likening it to 'an elongated cigarette lighter'.

Pevsner may have damned Lee-on-the-Solent's ballroom, cinema and viewing tower with faint praise, but its arrival in 1935 had marked a new chapter for the resort. Its opening came a few years after a fire, sparked by an electrical fault, had destroyed the pier pavilion. No one was injured in the blaze which happened on a quiet Sunday afternoon in June, but by the time firemen arrived the only thing they could do was to try to prevent the flames from spreading. Demolishing part of the decking, crowds, among them members of the Harvey Lawrence Dance Band, who lost all their instruments in the inferno, gathered on the seafront to watch the disaster unfold. Those who had been planning to go to a tea dance in the pavilion that afternoon counted their

blessings that the blaze hadn't started an hour or so later, and all watched as the much-loved venue turned into a charred wreck.

The loss of the pavilion was a huge blow for the resort and the promise of a new entertainment venue was not only vital economically, but, embracing a new style of architecture, it was also aesthetically important. The Lee Tower complex was to be built in the Art Deco style, its clean lines far removed from the imposing Victorian homes on Marine Parade.

'Lee was at something of a crossroads,' says local historian John Green. 'The town was divided between those who wanted it to remain a quiet residential haven and those who wanted to push forward with plans to turn it into a seaside resort. A group of local businessmen got together and, inspired by what had happened elsewhere in the country, started to draw up plans for a major entertainment complex on the seafront. Obviously by this stage a lot of resorts were already well-established, so if it was going to work it needed to make a big impression.'

Designed in the shape of a Y, it boasted of being a state-of-the-art entertainment complex. On one side was a ballroom, on the other a cinema, and the first floor was home to the Palm Court café and restaurant. From above, it was supposed to replicate a huge ocean liner – the recently launched *Queen Mary*. The pier was to be the stern, the cinema and ballroom the bridge. Opposite, a grand hotel was to

Previous pages: The waters of Lee-on-the-Solent witnessed a number of historic events. Eight years after playing a part in D-Day, RAF sea planes, led by Captain W.H. Pulford, arrived home after successfully flying 14,000 miles from Cairo to the Cape and back.

Opposite: Lee Tower, photographed in 1955, some twenty years after building work was completed on the complex, which brought Art Deco glamour to the resort.

'The town was divided between those who wanted it to remain a quiet residential haven and those who wanted to push forward with plans to turn it into a seaside resort.'

conform to the shape of the bow and on top was to be mounted a bust whose face was that of the *Queen Mary*'s captain. However, it was what was at the centre that drew the most attention – a 120ft tower from whose viewing platform it was possible to see miles across the Solent.

Those who passed the building site in the first few months of the construction could have been forgiven for thinking that the striking artist impressions they'd seen in the local paper would never emerge from the mud and rubble.

In fact it was almost destroyed before it was built when a gas cylinder fell from the top tower. A quick-thinking workman prevented an explosion by covering it with sand and then, brick by brick, the two-storey building began to emerge. When the white rendering was complete, it looked as if a ship and lighthouse had somehow been washed ashore.

It was Boxing Day 1935 when the complex was officially opened and all who took their seats in the new cinema to watch the Sonnie Hale farce, *Marry the Girl* and *Be Mine Tonight* agreed that it was the best Christmas present the town could have asked for.

The author of the souvenir programme handed out to guests that evening didn't hold back either: 'The cinema forms part of one of the most magnificent and imposing edifices in the South of England, which in the near future will be known throughout the country. Its origin is entirely due to the enterprise and courage displayed by the chairman of Solent Properties Ltd ... who, seeing the outstanding position of Lee-on-the-Solent as a modern seaside resort, determined to build such a structure that any king would be pleased to claim as theirs ... it need hardly be added, that it will remain as a monument of craftsmanship and energy ... for all time.'

When the railway carried its first 1,000 visitors into Lee-on-the-Solent, it had promised to transport them to the place 'where the rainbow ends'. With the opening of the new tower, its transformation from farmland to a modern seaside resort had been completed in less than half a century.

Much as the pier and the pavilion had been, the complex became the heart and soul of the town. In its first year of opening, takings for food, drink and cigarettes came to more than £7,000, but it was not enough and part of the problem was down to its design. Just ten people at a time could squeeze on to the viewing platform and, with a maximum of four people in the lift, visitors were often disappointed when they were ushered down after just a few minutes to make room for more.

Accepting they were never going to make a fortune from the tower itself, the management instead ploughed their efforts into the ballroom and cinema. Just twelve months or so after its official opening, it was repainted in camouflage colours to minimise the chance of it being it hit during Second World War bombing raids. However, inside the dances and the film screenings continued as usual.

'My Mum used to tell me how, when the air raid sirens went off, any military who were in the cinema used to get up and leave, but everyone else stayed put,' says marine artist Colin Baxter, who now lives in Gosport, just down the road from his childhood home in Lee. 'They knew the tower was a landmark for the German bombers. They used it to help plot the location of the coastal military bases and so it was unlikely to be a target. In fact, whenever a siren went off, they reckoned the cinema was probably the safest place to be.'

In the lead-up to the D-Day landings, the US Navy moved into Lee Tower. As the Solent filled with ships belonging to the Allied forces, at the nearby airfield Spitfires, Mustangs and Typhoons from the Fleet Air Arm were sent on reconnaissance missions over the beaches of Normandy. The assault had been due to take place in May 1944, but was delayed by a month to allow more troops to gather. Inside Lee Tower, the Americans carefully plotted their own role in Operation Overlord and on 6 June thousands of ships crossed the Channel in what was the largest amphibious invasion ever launched.

While Lee may have played a crucial role in the events of 1944, even a cursory glance at the accounts showed that the town was never destined to remain the same resort where, a few years earlier, thousands had flocked to see Flight Lieutenant Staniforth break the air speed record when he calmly notched up an average speed of 408.8mph in the skies above Lee.

Just two years after the complex had opened, the Lee Tower Company had gone into liquidation and, while the ballroom, cinema and restaurants were taken over by various other outfits, it was a sign of just how difficult making money was going to be.

Elsewhere in the town, the outdoor heated swimming pool was also struggling. It, too, had opened in the 1930s, but even in its early years attendance figures had not met expectations. Various alternatives were put forward, but it wasn't long before the pool was filled in and turned into a children's playground. The end was also nigh for the Art Deco tower.

'I had some fabulous times there,' says Colin. 'We all did. Lee was a fabulous place to grow up. It seemed to have everything, but then it all just disappeared. It was a funny time; I think there was a general feeling within the council that historically Lee had received much more investment than the rest of the area, but in attempting to redress the balance the town really lost out. The other major change was a massive house-building project. That really altered the atmosphere of the place. It no longer felt like a resort, it was just a town beside the sea.'

The tower stood as a testament to Lee-on-the-Solent's grand ambitions not for eternity, but for just thirty-six years. By the time the bulldozers moved in during 1971, what remained of the pier had already been demolished and Lee-on-the-Solent's conversion from popular seaside resort to residential town began. Today, there are no big hotels. They have all been converted into flats or been replaced by retirement homes. All that remains of the tower complex is the Remembrance Gardens.

'Many don't even realise there was anything ever there,' says Colin. 'It's funny, there was a bus stop just in front of the tower and it was freezing because it was always in the shadow. When the tower was demolished you no longer had to put your coat on to wait for the bus, but I think most of us would have endured a few more goose pimples if there had been some way to save the old place.'

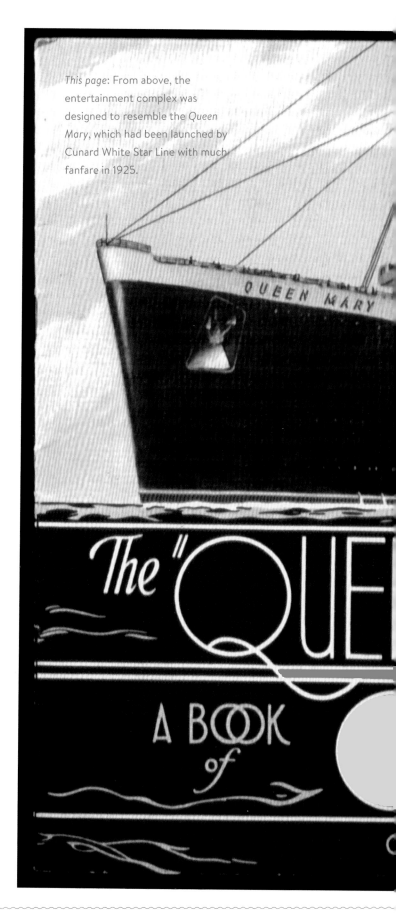

This page: From above, the entertainment complex was designed to resemble the *Queen Mary*, which had been launched by Cunard White Star Line with much fanfare in 1925.

THE FIRST CUNARDER "BRITANNIA" TOGETHER WITH THE THREE SHIPS WITH WHICH COLUMBUS FIRST CROSSED THE ATLANTIC COULD BE PLACED IN THE MAIN FOYER *and* RESTAURANT of *The* "QUEEN MARY"

N MARY" COMPARISONS

NARD WHITE STAR LINE

M A R

G A T E

Some people associate the seaside with a certain smell, the unmistakable aroma of cockles drenched in vinegar, perhaps, or golden brown doughnuts fresh from the fryer. Not Dominic Savage. For him it's all about sound, more specifically the distant echo of an organ carried on the breeze along Margate's seafront. For forty years his father, Tony, was the man who provided the music at the lido, the resort's vast entertainment complex.

He was there every day without fail during the summer season and whenever Dominic returns to his home town and walks past the empty space where the lido once stood, amid the sound of the seagulls and the waves rushing on to the sands, he can still make out the strains of 'Whatever Will Be Will Be' and 'The Yellow Rose of Texas'.

'I can't think of Margate without hearing my Dad's music,' says Dominic, now a successful film and television director living in London. 'He did three sessions a day – morning, afternoon and evening – and there would be two thousand people packed into the place. It was a simple thing, really. He would play, they would sing along. He also encouraged them to send up requests. They'd scribble a song on a piece of paper, often to celebrate a wedding or anniversary, and it felt very personal because it was. Sometimes they would sing, often very badly, but it didn't matter, people loved it.'

During their week's stay, some of those holidaymakers rarely ventured much further than the lido. They didn't need to. Aside from the semi-circular pool, holding up to 1,000 bathers, and the large amphitheatre where Tony also organised the ballroom dancing, there were hairdressing salons, ice cream parlours, and the countless bars and cafés brought the rest of the world to the Kent coast. One had a Caribbean theme, another was French and a third, called the Golden Garter Saloon, was home to an American Wild West show.

'Every lunchtime the cowboys would stage a mock shoot-out in the lido to advertise the matinee performance,' says Dominic, who spent most of his summer holidays there. 'Why did Margate have a Wild West show? Who knows, but it did and it seemed a perfectly normal way to spend an afternoon.

'Those were the days when people not only went to the same place for their summer holiday, but they stayed in the same guesthouse at exactly the same time of year and they did exactly the same things. I remember Dad would turn to me and say, "Right, it's Yorkshire week this week" or "It'll be Birmingham week in a fortnight" and he was never wrong.

Previous pages: Two little girls enjoying a lollipop while keeping cool in the waters of Margate Lido in the summer of 1961.

Left: John Boys built Margate's very first bathhouse, which was remodelled in the 1920s into an entertainment complex.

Opposite: During the 1920s and 1930s, swimming became incredibly popular in Britain, thanks in part to new swimwear designs, and the lido capitalised on the craze.

'He really looked forward to seeing certain families again. Dad was part of their holidays. He was the man who played the organ and who organised the old-time and modern dancing in the space between the deckchairs and the stage. To be honest, there wasn't really enough room, but no one seemed to mind. You'd have sixty couples doing the foxtrot from between 11a.m. and 12.30p.m. They'd go back to the hotel for lunch and be back on the dot of 2.45p.m. for another session. People were creatures of habit in those days and when they came to Margate, many of them spent most of their week in a deckchair in the lido listening to Dad.'

When Tony arrived in Margate in the 1950s, after serving in the RAF and a spell living in Paris, the lido had been open for less than two decades. However, the resort's association with watery pursuits can be traced back much further.

Margate had been at the forefront of sea-bathing ever since the early eighteenth century when a number of leading doctors had become convinced saltwater could alleviate everything from gout to bronchitis. Not everyone was persuaded by the healing properties of Britain's coastal waters, however. In fact, a significant section of the medical profession had a deep mistrust of the sea, believing immersion could both trigger lascivious thoughts and expose deeply buried perversions in even the most outwardly upstanding members of polite society. The science behind the claims was never quite explained and the naysayers were largely ignored by the well-heeled who headed to the coast en masse.

'The search for better health led people to the coast,' says architectural historian Kathryn Ferry, who can justifiably claim to be a world expert on bathing and beach huts, having visited more than 20,000 of them. 'First cold water, then saltwater were promoted as miracle cures and by the eighteenth century the wealthy were prepared to travel long distances over poor roads for a dip in the medicinal ocean.'

Margate had been at the forefront of sea-bathing ever since the early eighteenth century when a number of leading doctors had become convinced saltwater could alleviate everything from gout to bronchitis.

In the early days, bathers were wheeled into the water on horse-drawn carts, but getting in and out of the sea with dignity wasn't always easy. It might well explain why Margate Quaker Benjamin Beale was moved to devise what he called the modesty hood. Effectively an awning attached to the back of the cart, once in the water the device was lowered over the bather, ensuring maximum privacy.

'You have to remember that not many people at this time could swim,' adds Kathryn. 'Their first introduction was likely to be in the hands of a guide paid to push their head repeatedly below the waves. It wasn't particularly dignified, so a little privacy was clearly beneficial. Beale's invention was quickly taken up and Margate's popularity as a resort increased as a result. Hiring a bathing machine was not cheap and, while it may seem odd now, they were a real status symbol.'

While health fads come and go, the British public's love affair with the sea showed no sign of abating and by the early decades of the nineteenth century a number of entrepreneurs were beginning to wonder how they might cash in on what was becoming a lucrative industry.

Among them was John Boys, an influential figure in Margate, who in 1824 began building the resort's first bathhouse. Excavating part of the cliffside for his Gothic-style fort, its large, domed, circular chamber had room for up to thirty bathing machines, now with their own changing rooms. The emphasis was still very much on sea-bathing, but within the bathhouse a tunnel also led down to a reservoir used by women and children as a plunge pool, believed to be the first of its kind in the country. Elsewhere, a large boiler room provided water for hot baths and alongside the bathing rooms – one for men and one

Opposite: Some didn't stray from the lido and after a day on the sun terraces, couples would return at night for an evening of dancing.

Right: Tony Savage played the organ at Margate Lido for forty years and taught his son Dominic some of his favourite tunes.

Below: Like many open-air pools, the lido wouldn't have been complete without the occasional beauty contest.

for women – there were also various reading rooms with a space for an organ and a billiard table. It might all sound terribly genteel, but those early fears for Britain's moral welfare had not quite gone away.

'[In] no town in England, and as far as my experience goes, on the Continent, can such utterly indecent exhibitions be daily witnessed as at Margate during bathing hours,' wrote one anonymous visitor in the letters pages of *The Times* in 1871. 'Nothing can be more revolting to persons having the least feelings of modesty than the promiscuous mixing of bathers, nude men dancing, swimming or floating with women, not quite nude certainly, but with scant clothing. Tide machines for males and females are not kept apart and the latter do not apparently care to keep within the awnings. The authorities post notices as to "indecent bathing", but that appears to be all they think they ought to do.'

The seaside had become a place to escape to, away from the normal rules of everyday life. Resorts like Margate represented freedom, a spirit immortalised in music hall songs like 'You Can Do Things at the Seaside (That you can't do in town)' by Charles Ridgewell and George Stevens:

Have you ever noticed when you're by the sea
The things that you can do there with impunity?
If you did the same things when you're up in town
Moral Mrs Grundy on her face would wear a frown,
Father, mother, all the family
Travel down to have a little paddle in the sea
Mother takes her stockings off upon the sandy shore
And shows a lot of linen that she'd never shown before.

Watch them at the seaside, there upon the sands,
Percy and his sweetheart hold each other's hands,
All among the crowd, there they will sit and spoon
Like a pair of turtle-doves upon a honeymoon,
There they loll beside the briny blue,
Cuddled up together till you can't tell who is who.
Canoodling and kissing with a crowd of people there,
No one seems to notice them and no one seems to care.

John Henry Iles, who also owned Margate's Dreamland amusement park, knew better than most what holidaymakers wanted, in the 1920s he began turning the baths into a modern entertainment complex.

'Before then, all focus had been on the pier with resorts building longer and longer structures,' says social historian Steven Braggs. 'However, resorts were always on the lookout for ways of tempting holidaymakers to their shores and lidos were out to become the next big thing. While it might seem odd that people were willing to pay to swim in an open-air pool when the sea was right next door, you have to remember the waters were quite heavily controlled. You had to pay to use a changing room and to hire a costume and towel and lidos were often cheaper. Also the water was filtered and tended to be at least a little warmer than the sea.

'Swimming was probably the first exercise craze in Britain and quite quickly every resort wanted its own lido.'

By the mid-1930s, a new open-air swimming pool and amphitheatre had been built on top of Boys's original bathhouse. Arranged over three terraces and rebranded as Margate Lido, it was surrounded by cafés and bars and was the envy of other resorts.

'The May Day bank holiday was when it all started,' says Dominic. 'From that day you could really start counting down to summer. It's hard to believe now, but there were so many people on the pavement that it took forever to get from one end of the resort to the other.'

Scattered among the ordinary families were a sprinkling of famous faces. *Oliver!* writer and composer Lionel Bart was a regular in Margate, as was Norman Wisdom, who would always pop over to the lido to perform a few songs with Tony Savage whenever he was in town, and occasionally Cynthia Payne, the suburban brothel madam, whose life story was later immortalised in the film *Personal Services*, was also spotted on the sun terrace.

'To have a dad who was so much part of the fabric of the place was really special and we had this routine which meant I got to share in it a little. At the end of one of his shows, I would go up as just another punter and hand over a request for "Twelfth Street Rag". It's a bit of a tricky jazz number and Dad would say, "I tell you what, why don't you have a go?". My feet could barely reach the pedals and of course none of the audience thought I could play. You could hear the gasps as I rattled through it. At the end Dad would ask for my name and as soon as I said, "Dominic, Dominic Savage", they were in on the joke.

Right: Norman Wisdom was a regular visitor to Margate, along with the composer Lionel Bart and celebrity madam Cynthia Payne.

'You know, I often thought he had the best job in the world. He gave so much pleasure to people, and when someone would come up to me and squeeze 50p into my hand or buy me a little present, I thought this isn't a bad way to earn a living.

'While his own family weren't at all musical, Dad had real talent and a way with the audience, but the one thing he lacked was ambition. I have no doubt he could have earned more money and got a more prestigious job, but he was happy in Margate; it suited him.'

By the time Dominic left for film school in the early 1980s, the sun had already set on the resort's heyday. The open-air swimming pool had closed at the end of the 1970s and when the lido's sun terraces were demolished in 1991, it seemed a final admission of defeat.

'In the past, three generations of the same family would go on holiday together, but you began to notice that the younger ones had stopped coming,' says Dominic. 'Eventually it was only the grandparents who were coming back to Margate. At that point you knew it was over.'

Dominic's dad kept on performing in other venues right up until his death in 2004. His mother passed away in 2009, and since then there have been big changes in Margate. The Turner Contemporary Art Gallery opened in 2011 and was billed as a catalyst for regeneration. In a little over two years, it attracted a million visitors and it's hoped its success will attract other creative industries to the town. Dominic hopes so too, but it's already a very different town from the one his parents knew.

'When I grew up people were living the real experience of the seaside town. It was a proper community. I'm not sure that's true now. People visit out of a sense of nostalgia, they like the idea of what it once was, rather than what it is now.'

R　　　E　　　D

C A R

When Redcar Beacon was officially opened in March 2013, the seaside resort was covered in a light dusting of snow and a biting wind was blowing in from the North Sea. Its name had been decided by a public vote – Lemon Top Tower and Mo's Lookout, the latter in memory of the town's late MP Mo Mowlam, both failing to make the cut – but on that wintry day, the project's working title, the Vertical Pier, still loomed large.

The 80ft-high structure is the centrepiece of a £75 million regeneration project, designed to house a café and provide affordable business space. Climb the 132 steps up to the viewing platform and one side looks across to a large wind farm. On the other are the Cleveland Hills. Lit up at night, the beacon is a striking addition to the seafront, yet its resemblance to an old-fashioned helter-skelter is about as close as it gets to conjuring the romance of Redcar's original pier, which, like so many of the other wooden structures across the country, was lost before anyone thought to save it.

'The concept of the pleasure pier originated out of the sheer difficulty of reaching the seaside watering places,' says architectural historian Lynn Pearson. 'Even with the arrival of quick, reliable steam passenger vessels around 1815, there was still the problem of how you transferred people from ship to shore. The very first piers were little more than narrow wooden jetties, but during the 1840s piers were no longer just purely functional. Visitors, attracted to the sea but repelled by its danger, could promenade along the pier in complete safety, yet still enjoy a frisson of excitement caused by being close to the waves below. The real boom in pier building began in the 1860s and it was really towards the end of the century that the original pavilions, built as shelters, started to be transformed into ornate palaces of entertainment.'

For those who were among the hundreds who packed into Redcar's pavilion for nightly dances during the pier's heyday in the 1950s, all that remains are the memories. Memories like those of Yvonne Vickers.

'I remember every detail of that night,' she says of a life-changing evening in 1958. 'I was wearing lots of net petticoats, rinsed in sugar water to make them so stiff they would stand out to the end of the evening, stiletto heels and, of course, Roman pink lipstick. There was a machine in the cloakroom where for a few pence you could get a good squirt of perfume, and a silver ball in the middle of the ceiling cast pretty patterns across the room. To me it always seemed the most romantic place in the world. I was seventeen and as soon as John asked me dance, that was it, I knew we were destined to be married.'

Previous page: When it opened in 1873, Redcar pier stretched 1,300ft into the sea and boasted a bandstand and seating for 700 people.

Left: Billy Scarrow (front, second from right) performed in a number of other pierrot troupes before arriving in Redcar.

Opposite: Seated here by the piano, Billy was the main provider of what he saw as good wholesome entertainment in the resort throughout the 1930s.

A whirlwind romance followed and when Yvonne and John got engaged, there was only one place to celebrate. Gathering together a group of friends and relatives, the couple again took to the floor of the pier pavilion as the Danny Mitchell Orchestra played on.

'Halfway through the night the big doors of the ballroom would open so you could walk outside on to the pier itself,' says Yvonne. 'The silvery moon was reflected in the sea and as the waves lapped quietly all around, you could still hear the strains of the band playing inside.

'The night we got engaged, my Mum asked the band to play "True Love".'

The song had been a hit for Grace Kelly and Bing Crosby in the film *High Society*, but Yvonne never heard the version dedicated to her and her fiancé.

'John and I were stood outside admiring the sea and missed the whole thing. Often after we'd been out on the pier, we'd go to the upstairs coffee bar to get warm. I know it seems dull and old-fashioned, but to me it was the most magical evening you could ever wish for.'

The fact the pier and the pavilion ballroom survived to provide a backdrop for Yvonne's engagement at all was something of a miracle. The 1,300ft-long structure, complete with bandstand and seating for 700, had only been open for seven years when in 1880 it was sliced in two by the Luna sailing brig. Repairs were quick, but disaster struck again five years later when a steamship, stranded on nearby rocks, broke free and smashed into the pier, carrying off the landing stage. Before the turn of the twentieth century, a fire also did its best to finish off the pier. Some would have taken these disasters as an omen, a sign that this stretch of the North Sea was too inhospitable for a pleasure pier. However, each time the pier seemed to come back stronger than before.

By the 1920s, with its newly-extended pavilion and ballroom, Redcar had become a premier east coast resort, second only to Scarborough. As the crowds descended on the sands, heading for the pier, they wanted to be entertained and if no one else was going to do it, William Henry Scarrow reckoned he would have a go.

His grandson Neil picks up the story: 'When Billy came back from the Great War he toured all over the UK with a troupe called Dixon's Crazy Town Revue; he appeared in pantomime in Blackpool and was cast in a number of films. So when he finally arrived back in his childhood home of Redcar he was already an experienced entertainer.'

By then, pierrot troupes, which had emerged towards the end of the nineteenth century, were

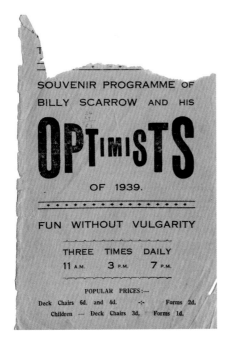

a familiar sight at Britain's seaside resorts, and the traditional white face paint and monochrome costumes had been replaced by boaters and blazers or evening dress.

In many ways Billy was a visionary, regularly finding himself pitched against those who seemed to want to preserve Redcar in aspic. Billy knew that wasn't an option. If Redcar opted for the status quo, it would gradually die as a resort.

It was why he set up his temporary stage as close as he could to the pier. Location was everything and that was why, one Friday evening in 1936, when inspectors, employed by the council, dispersed the large crowd watching Billy perform, the ensuing row made it to the pages of the *Cleveland Standard*.

'If Redcar is to keep pace with other resorts it must have other attractions than glorious heritage,' Billy was reported to have said. 'The sands are ideal for children, but older people want other things as well. Redcar should be careful not to thwart enterprise and allow it to become a dead town.'

Billy did persist. His troupe performed three shows a day every summer between 1931 and 1939. He became adept at dealing with the more raucous elements of the crowd and on occasion was known to stop his performance for a few minutes while he acted as official ejector to his own show.

The line-up would change each season, but over the years the troupe included a male impersonator, comedian, banjo player, violinist and one year a man described as both a yodeller and an eccentric dancer. It was a show dubbed 'fun without the vulgarity' and, while the early years were hard, by 1935 Billy was employing fourteen people on a decent living wage.

The outbreak of war marked the end of the Redcar Pierrots and it would also change the pier forever.

'The Second World War was especially disastrous for piers on the south and east coast and Redcar, like many others, was deliberately breached to prevent it being used as a landing stage,' says Lynn. 'After the end of the war, the surviving piers were returned tattered and broken to their owners and while some financial compensation was available it wasn't really until the 1980s that people began to appreciate Victorian architecture, and in many places there simply wasn't the appetite for restoration.'

Cut in two, a stray mine had further weakened Redcar's once great pier and by the time the war

Above: As this scene shows, the 1950s were a boom-time for Redcar, which was often packed with holidaymakers who saw the seaside as an escape from the austerity of the post-war years.

was over only a short section remained. Fortunately, it was the part that was home to the ballroom and the 1950s did mark something of a revival for the pavilion's fortunes. Like Yvonne and John, it was where hundreds of couples met, but as the years ticked on, even the gloss of romance couldn't mask the peeling paint or the growing cracks in both the 80ft pier and the pavilion.

By the 1960s, most agreed that both had seen better days. Where once 400 people had attended the weekend dances, by 1967 it was down to just 150 and there was a definite hollow echo as the Danny Mitchell Orchestra did its best to play on. The pier was on the point of bankruptcy, but such was the emotional attachment that even when rough seas lifted the ballroom floor out of its retaining bolts, the people of

Redcar refused to let it fall into a watery grave.

The money was found for repairs and when the Cleveland Organ Society announced it was interested in installing a 6-tonne Wurlitzer in the pavilion, it seemed it might be possible to breathe new life into the old place. The optimism lasted just eighteen months. In 1979, the council laid bare the figures. To repair the pier would cost £185,000. To demolish it would cost £30,000. This time there was no room for sentimentality. In December 1980, what remained of the pier was dismantled.

'Ironically, the destruction of Redcar pier signalled something of a sea change and by the end of the decade the restoration of Britain's piers was greeted with enthusiasm by the public and became acceptable to funding bodies,' says Lynn. 'Britain's piers blurred the distinction between engineering and architecture, but by the time their timeless appeal was recognised and preservation trusts were set up to safeguard their future, many had already been consigned to history.'

Opposite above: At its height of popularity, hundreds attended weekend dances, but by the 1970s when this photograph was taken, the ballroom's heyday was over.

Opposite below: Many hoped the arrival of the Wurlitzer in the late 1970s, seen here being repaired by Robin Roper, would safeguard the pier's future.

This page: Redcar's new vertical pier opened in 2013 as part of a major regeneration of the town, but its design has proved controversial.

JAY W

VICK

There are some league tables that no town wants to top. Back in 2010, Jaywick was named the most deprived place in the country and even reading the fine print of the detailed report there was little sign of hope. Individually, statistics on employment prospects, health, disability, crime and living standards were grim. Together, they painted a picture of a place that had slipped through the net, a place which was difficult, awkward and perhaps best forgotten.

By way of contrast, Chorleywood, in Hertfordshire, less than a 100-mile-drive away, was ranked as the least deprived. Properties there cost thirty times as much as Jaywick where 62 per cent of the working-age population relied on benefits and where securing a mortgage wasn't top of most people's priorities.

Yet those figures don't tell the whole picture.

They don't tell of the ingenuity of one man who believed he could turn bleak marshland into a thriving resort. They don't tell of the community spirit which fought off successive attempts to bulldoze the place, and they don't tell how for a while this small corner of Essex was once a little piece of paradise for working class Londoners.

It was a cold winter's morning in 1928 when Frank Stedman motored down to the coast to show his solicitor and bank manager an old farm, the location for his new seaside resort. With sleet obscuring the view and a bleak wind whistling along the coast, it wasn't a day to linger, but nothing could dissuade Frank from his ambitious plans.

'It had started to snow again and the people with me got back into the car, shuddering and saying, "Thank goodness we have seen the last of that",' he later remembered. 'I disagreed. I said, "I will buy the farm". I did so, and thought "I am glad to have seen it under the worst possible conditions; I can visualise it in the sunshine".'

Where others saw remote marshland, he saw tree-lined avenues, landscaped gardens, tennis lawns, sports grounds running down to the sea and a church named St Christopher's, after the patron saint of travellers. He also had plans for 'fine bathing houses' which could be bought for £25 each, a dance hall and a mile-long lake for motorboat racing and water polo.

Even when that last project proved a spectacular and very public failure when the water drained away as quickly as it was poured in, Frank's enthusiasm was undiminished and there were plenty of newly mobile Londoners ready to ride the crest of the wave with him.

While others would have seen insurmountable problems, he saw only opportunities. So when the council denied him planning permission to build permanent houses in one part of the estate, citing genuine issues with drainage, Frank instead said he

Previous pages: The development at Jaywick was the brainchild of Frank Stedman, who never wavered in his determination to turn bleak marshland into a thriving resort.

Left: Jaywick, where every chalet came with a parking space, was dubbed a 'Motorist's Mecca by the Sea.'

Opposite: While most arrived under their own steam, for those without cars there were regular coach services to the town.

EASTERN ⬤ NATIONAL
OMNIBUS COMPANY LIMITED

Regular
COACH SERVICES
TILBURY, GRAYS
AND
CLACTON, JAYWICK SANDS
LOWESTOFT & YARMOUTH
BOOK HERE

EASTERN NATIONAL

FOR COMFORT, CONVENIENCE AND ECONOMY

This page: The facilities might not have been luxurious, but as countless holiday snaps showed, for many Jaywick Sands was a welcome escape from the smog-filled capital.

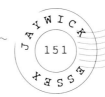

The Beach, Jaywick   10567

With every chalet having room to park a car, Jaywick Sands marketed itself as a 'Motorist's Mecca by the Sea'

would build more beach huts, the kind the authorities assumed would only be used by day-trippers.

'I sometimes feel that he used up the family's stores of energy,' says his grandson Neil Stedman, who many years later would take over the management of the Jaywick Estate. 'He'd been a developer for a number of years before he settled at the coast and he always had some new project on the go. Not all of them worked out, but you couldn't fault his ambition or his enthusiasm. He recognised that there was a new car-owning demographic and really he built Jaywick for them.'

With every chalet having room to park a car, Jaywick Sands marketed itself as a 'Motorist's Mecca by the Sea' and workers from the Ford plant in Dagenham were among the first arrivals, unpacking their suitcases in streets named after the Hillman, Wolseley and Bentley.

As one advertisement in the *London Star* in 1932 put it: 'It is a place which while offering petrol and oil, food and electricity, light, telephones and other essentials for civilisation, gives rippling sea and silvery sands, ocean breezes and absolute freedom from inhibiting restrictions.'

For the first time the seaside holiday was open to families from London on moderate incomes and they didn't need to be asked twice. Some bought the finished article, while others invested in a plot of land, ferrying the materials to build their own des res from the capital. All felt part of an exciting adventure.

'In the first half of the twentieth century a unique landscape emerged along the coast ... more reminiscent of the American frontier than of the traditionally well-ordered English landscape,' wrote the late Colin Ward in his book *Arcadia for All* (written with Dennis Hardy). 'It was a makeshift

world of shacks and shanties, scattered unevenly in plots of varying shapes and sizes, with unmade roads and little in the way of services. To the local authorities who dubbed this type of landscape the plotlands, it was something of a nightmare, an anarchic rural slum. But to the plotlanders themselves, Arcadia was born. At a cost of only a few pounds, ordinary city dwellers discovered not only fresh air and tranquility, but most important of all, a sense of freedom.'

Looking back on the first five years, even Frank admitted surprise at the pace of the development.

'The first two dozen pioneers have often said they thought they had found a kind of Robinson Crusoe island where they could be quiet and peaceful and enjoy the difficulties of going to the farmhouse for the well water. But they did not realise the fact that once started, so many others would find out themselves the healthful air and the advantages of the district.'

Bernard Mann remembers the feeling well.

'My Granddad ran a business in London and he bought a house on the Tudor Estate and for a while he would spend winters in the city and summers at the coast,' says the retired deputy head teacher. 'When I was a kid we would have a trunk sent down ahead of us and then me, Mum and my half-brothers and sisters would get the coach down.

'We lived in Wembley and I will always remember the smell of the countryside. You forget how industrial and smog-filled London was. Sometimes now when I get up on a morning, I smell that exact same smell and I'm instantly transported back to those early family holidays.'

For those who spent fifty-one weeks a year breathing in the polluted air of the capital, it didn't matter that at Jaywick Sands water had to be collected from a standpipe or that the early morning alarm was the sound of the lorry responsible for emptying the chemical toilets.

'We used a chalet that belonged to a friend of my Mum who worked at the same Wimpy Bar,' says

Opposite: Jaywick might not have been the prettiest resort, but it did cater for a growing number of working-class holidaymakers.

Doreen Patterson. 'It was basic, but so was life back home. We used to drive down there in my elder brother's car, packed to the roof it was. We'd even take the television. Often we'd break down or get a flat tyre on the way and everything we owned would end up unpacked by the side of the road. But it didn't matter how long it took, getting there was the important thing. You know, I even used to look forward to going to get the water from the pump at the end of the road; it seemed a bit exotic.'

The Jaywick Sands development Frank Stedman imagined was never intended to win any architectural prizes, but even those inclined to look down their noses a little at the hotchpotch nature of the chalets couldn't help but find at least some merit in the enterprise.

'I found this extraordinary piece of holiday shack development surprising and rather interesting in a way, though it does leave one perhaps with a feeling of nausea about it all,' wrote one civil servant, who was helping to compile a survey of coastal towns during the Second World War. 'There are many hundreds of wooden shacks erected without proper regard for the right use of materials or proper layout, but it is an inescapable fact that the colony does provide for many thousands of holidaymakers each year to enjoy a holiday by the sea.'

Those who braved the traffic jams on the A133 didn't ask for much from their holiday. Most were content with watching a Punch and Judy show on the sands or playing cards on tables set up along the front, before grabbing fish and chips from the beach café. In Jaywick there was to be no grand theatre, no winter gardens or pleasure park. Instead, Stedman erected a marquee where on summer evenings a local trio called the Jolly Three Jays would play, and close by the Morocco Club was the start and finish of the resort's nightlife.

The nearest Jaywick Sands got to a tourist attraction was a miniature railway. It had been the idea of Frank's son, Reginald, and was designed to connect the resort with Crossways station a mile or so away. Opened in 1936, the green and cream painted carriages with their plush interiors and electric lighting were arguably more luxurious than many of the holiday chalets. Operating seven days a week, it carried 2,000 passengers a day during the summer, but it wasn't to last. When war came,

Jaywick Sands went into hibernation, the line was dismantled and the mile of metal tracks melted down for ammunition.

As London's largely working class East End took a hammering from nightly bombing raids, many of those who had built their own holiday chalets decided to move permanently to the coast. Almost overnight, Jaywick turned from a seaside resort into a residential coastal town and, as tastes became more sophisticated, its lack of running water and the chemical toilets, once seen as somehow quaintly charming, now put off all but the resort's most dedicated holidaymakers.

'We were among a lot of people who ended up moving there permanently,' says Bernard. 'It was 1959, I was eleven years old and to me it felt like being on holiday all the time, particularly as it took about three months to sort out a school. In London I'd had to get the Tube every day. I hated it. Suddenly I could go to the beach every day.'

While Bernard, and others like him, were grateful to have escaped the grime of home, the shift was causing a headache for the local authority.

The Brooklands and Grasslands area of the town had never been meant to house a permanent population and the chalets, some fashioned from packing crates from the Dagenham factory, were, according to the council, eyesores in need of demolition. In 1971, there was an attempt at a compulsory purchase order on the grounds that the two estates were both dilapidated and unsanitary. Only a minority of the property owners were swayed by the £200 compensation package. Those ninety chalets were duly bulldozed, but the rest stood defiant and whatever hope the council had that it would eventually get its way eventually fizzled out.

Before the Second World War, it had been estimated that 97 per cent of Jaywick's floating population were holidaymakers and just 3 per cent were permanent residents. By 1986, the ratio had been reversed. The following year, the Morocco Club closed and by then those who ran the fairground rides had already moved on. In their place came large pockets of social deprivation and high unemployment. Many in Jaywick felt ignored by both local and national government, but, while some began new lives elsewhere, most stayed.

'When it became clear it was moving towards permanent occupation, the council never did grab the nettle,' says Neil. 'If they had, things might have turned out differently. In 1971, had they offered to pay the current value of the properties, which was around £600, rather than the site value they might have had a different response and they might have been able to redevelop the area. They didn't and for many it felt like just another incident of the council ignoring those who live in Jaywick.

'There's a fierce loyalty to the place and over the years that's what they haven't really understood.'

Jaywick's days as a popular resort lasted no more than forty years and the town is now trying to find a new direction.

'The town hasn't had an easy time over the last few years, but we're still here and we're still fighting,' says Bernard. 'It might not be the resort that Frank Stedman imagined all those years ago, but I wouldn't want to live anywhere else.'

Above: For those who spent most of the year working in factories, Jaywick Sands represented freedom.

Opposite: The town was ranked as the most deprived place in the country in 2010, but many still hold happy memories of the place.

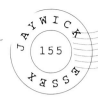

M O R E C

CAMBE

'Morecambe could have got by without my dad and I,' says Eric Smith, who in the 1940s brought one of the resort's most unusual attractions to life. 'But I like to think we were the icing on the cake.'

He is nostalgic with good reason. Now living just a few miles out of the town centre, he witnessed first-hand the rise and fall of the resort, which turn-of-the-twentieth-century tourist guides had called the Naples of the North because of its sheltered position and abundant supply of spring water.

By the 1950s, thanks to the large number of textile workers who headed there from West Yorkshire, it had become known less exotically as Bradford-on-Sea – so cherished was their patronage, the seafront shops even stocked their local *Telegraph* and *Argus* newspapers. Fast-forward a few decades and most called it Mucky Morecambe. It wasn't because of the souvenir shops selling kiss-me-quick hats and saucy seaside postcards, but a nod to the mudflats where the sand should have been. When the tide was out, some said they seemed to stretch as far as New York.

Call it what you will, to Eric the Lancashire resort, which once boasted two piers, eight cinemas, four dance halls and was flanked at either end by fairgrounds, has always been home. Today the piers have gone, the eight cinemas have been reduced to one and the adrenalin-fuelled screams of those who rode the Stampede roller coaster were silenced some years ago. Eric, though, still has his memories.

His own story began in an ordinary terraced house where his father's imagination brought light and colour into a world dimly lit by gas lamps. During the day, Frank Smith drove coaches, but he was also a keen amateur engineer and on evenings and weekends he would spend hours in his small workshop designing and building rides destined for Morecambe's Winter Gardens fairground, where coconut shies, waltzer and dodgems were already attracting holidaymakers in their thousands.

As soon as he was old enough, it was also where Eric would spend his summer holidays working for a man everyone knew as One-Armed Jack. Rumour had it he had lost his arm on a motorcycle wall of death. He hadn't. He'd been injured in a horse riding accident, but, quietly revelling in being a stuntman with a story to tell, Jack never bothered to correct the stories.

On quiet days, Eric would also help out at the circus. Among the attractions it boasted the world's smallest horse, which Eric would occasionally ride home if he didn't fancy the walk.

'It never really felt like work. To me the fairground was always like an extension of home. You knew everyone and everyone knew you.'

While he often watched his father tinkering with some new ride, Eric never had any particular plans to follow in his footsteps. Not until 1947, that is, when his parents returned home from a day at Belle Vue Zoo and Amusement Park in Manchester.

'They'd seen a real elephant giving children rides and my dad's imagination just ran away with him.'

Heading out to his workshop, Frank began building his own mechanical version destined to make a big impression on the Morecambe seafront.

'At that point I'd lost a bit of interest in the rides. I was fed up with working nights at the fairgrounds and had got a job as a motor mechanic, but when Dad started building his elephant, curiosity got the better of me.'

A week later, Eric peeked into his father's workshop. In the middle was a chassis, soon to be powered by an Austin Seven engine. It might not have looked much, but it was the beginnings of Jumbo, the mechanical elephant.

'Dad was always inventing things and no one took him very seriously, but the elephant was different. I knew that I could probably make him look a bit more lifelike and in the end it became a joint project.'

Using whatever materials were to hand, Eric fashioned the elephant's toes out of seashells, a local dentist donated some barrage balloon fabric for the hide and a windscreen wiper motor was adapted to make the eyes roll and the ears flap.

'We used to charge sixpence a time and there was always a long queue for a ride. It even had its own number plate and I remember one Saturday afternoon, as I was guiding it along the promenade, being warned by the police. I wasn't quite sixteen at the time and they thought I ought to have a licence to be in charge of a mechanical elephant.'

The ride was so successful that Frank eventually sold the patent to a company with the resources to manufacture a whole herd of the mechanical creatures. Jumbo was retired, but the Smiths remained at the heart of Morecambe's tourist

THE NEW LUXURY SWIMMING POOL

MORECAMBE AND HEYSHAM

BRITAIN'S MOST MODERN AND PROGRESSIVE RESORT

EXPRESS SERVICES AND CHEAP TICKETS BY L M S

OFFICIAL HOLIDAY GUIDE FROM ADVERTISING MANAGER, TOWN HALL, MORECAMBE.

Previous pages: The Lancashire resort became known as Bradford-on-Sea thanks to the number of holidaymakers from Yorkshire.

Above: Morecambe's Super Swimming Stadium welcomed its first bathers in 1936 and the attraction featured on much of the resort's advertising material.

'*I know when you look back you tend to only remember the good times and ignore the bad,*' says Eric. '*But there was always a sense of fun about Morecambe. It didn't take itself too seriously.*'

This page: The Morecambe
Winter Gardens had opened as
The Victoria Pavilion theatre in
1897 and was home to one of the
resort's main fairgrounds.

Built to capitalise on a swimming boom sweeping across the country, the sleek lines of the huge Art Deco lido screamed that Morecambe was a modern, fashionable resort.

business, running the miniature railway at the Winter Gardens. However, times were changing.

'In the old days people were happy to buy a jug of tea and two cups for a shilling and take it across to the beach for a picnic,' says Eric. 'But eventually that started to seem a little old-fashioned and so did the fairground.'

The Winter Gardens and its theatre, where the likes of George Formby and the 4ft 3in comic Jimmy Clitheroe, known throughout his career as the Clitheroe Kid, had performed, closed in 1977, and while a preservation trust has been desperately trying to secure funding for a major restoration project, the money hasn't yet been forthcoming. Whatever happens, the old fairground, which has been a car park for as long as most people can remember, is unlikely to be resurrected.

'I know when you look back you tend to only remember the good times and ignore the bad,' says Eric. 'But there was always a sense of fun about Morecambe. It didn't take itself too seriously.'

The sense of fun Eric talks about was embodied in one of Morecambe's most ambitious projects. The Super Swimming Stadium opened in July 1936 and it lived up to its name. Built to capitalise on a swimming boom sweeping across the country, the Art Deco lido screamed that Morecambe was a modern, fashionable resort.

'In the 1930s, outdoor pursuits like hiking and rambling became fashionable and magazines of the time were full of references to improving health and general fitness through swimming,' says Steven Braggs, a historian specialising in the popular culture of the twentieth century. 'The original bathing costumes had been designed to cover up as much of the body as possible and for women that had meant a full-length gown with weights sewn in the hem to keep it from rising in the water. However, in 1929 the American company Jantzen launched its new costumes with the slogan "the suit that changed bathing into swimming". They looked not unlike today's swimming costumes and it really was crucial in the development of the sport.

'As the swimming craze took hold, Morecambe

Left: Punch and Judy shows were a staple part of the Great British seaside. This one from 1939 entertained children with a version of Snow White and the Seven Dwarves.

Opposite: The pool proved instantly popular. Within the first two days of opening, 20,000 people had passed through the turnstiles.

Council decided it needed a large outdoor pool to compete with nearby Blackpool, and the site of the former ship-breaking business of T.W. Ward Ltd was ripe for redevelopment.'

Accommodating up to 1,200 bathers and 3,000 spectators, like the Midland Hotel, completed four years earlier, the Super Swimming Stadium was a shrine to that most modern of materials – concrete. Those behind the project talked of how 450 tons of steel, 400 lights and twelve miles of electrical wiring had gone into its construction. The figures were largely meaningless to the public, but they were enough to hint at Morecambe's scale of ambition. The first day it opened a mile-long queue snaked around the side of the stadium. Forty-eight hours later, 20,000 people had dipped their toes in the water. With the heating system not introduced until the following year, most found it cold, icy even. Not that it mattered. The stadium itself

became a focal point for visitors, and those daring enough to brave one of the high diving boards quickly became local celebrities.

One of them was a young boy called Barrie Wood who was recruited by the Marksway Swimwear Company to demonstrate their unsinkable suits. On one memorable day, Barrie grew bored with simply diving into the water. Instead, on one of the high boards he stepped into a sack and asked an able assistant to tie his hands and feet with rope. Once the top of the sack was secured, Barrie was pushed into the water. A minute or so later he returned to the surface and the crowd, which, like Barrie had been holding its breath, broke out into applause.

As the country emerged from the shadows of the Second World War, the Super Swimming Stadium was a glamorous alternative to economic austerity. In the summer of 1945, a group of young women in swimming costumes and high heels gathered at the

side of the pool. They were the first contestants in the resort's inaugural Bathing Beauty Contest.

The weather wasn't kind. Yet, despite having to huddle under umbrellas, the final was watched by a 4,300-strong audience. By the 1950s, Morecambe and its Super Swimming Stadium had become the focus of every would-be beauty queen. The prizes were generous – one year first place came with a cheque for £1,000, a diamond watch, a holiday for two in Ibiza and a pen set – but more importantly it also brought opportunity. Success in the north west resort could open doors into the world of both modelling and TV. One of the early winners was the first female *Blue Peter* presenter Leila Williams, and until Eric Morley set up his own feeder competition – a move that Morecambe challenged unsuccessfully in the courts – the winner was also guaranteed a place in the ultimate pageant – Miss World.

'When the Morecambe Corporation started the contest, they introduced to the attractions of holidays a new form of entertainment which has now become a big part of show business,' began the

official programme for the 1962 competition. 'As the years go by the size of the audience shows no signs of diminishing, the standard of our beautiful competitors improves steadily and the contest remains as popular as ever.'

At one time or another the event had boasted Bob Monkhouse, the actress Glynis Johns and Laurel and Hardy among its judges, and winners were guaranteed significant press coverage.

'Parading in front of a group of guesthouse landlords and ladies does all sound a little old-fashioned now, but then it was an accepted route into show business,' says Dinah May, who was crowned Miss Great Britain in Morecambe in 1976. 'My mother was a secretary, but she wanted a different life for me and it was her who really pushed me into entering the contests. I remember exactly what I wore for the finals that year. Previously I'd spent a lot of money on dresses and I'd decided I wasn't going to do that again. Instead I pulled on an old purple Grecian-style dress I had in the back of the wardrobe. My Mum was horrified.

Opposite left: Leila Williams, from Ellesmere Port, took first prize in the 1957 contest, with June Dawson and Margaret Rowe named runners-up.

Opposite right: In 1955, crowds at the Super Swimming Stadium watched Jennifer Chimes, from Leamington Spa, walk away with the main prize.

Right: Dinah May, who later became Michael Winner's PA, was named Miss Great Britain in 1976.

'Parading in front of a group of old guesthouse landlords and ladies does all sound a little old-fashioned now, but then it was an accepted route into show business.' DINAH MAY

'Some of the girls were so good at lip-reading that we often knew who had won before the judges announced the results. Not this time. The name of the girl I thought was going to win was called out in second place. I still remember now how nervous I was. My legs felt like jelly. When the head judge said my name I just burst into tears and all I could hear was my mother, who had been sat just to the right of the catwalk, screaming.'

By the time Dinah, who would later become PA to the film director Michael Winner, was choosing the mink jacket as part of her prize and seeing her picture in the paper under the headline 'Weeping Beauty', a little of Morecambe's glamorous past had already been erased. Just a few months earlier the Super Swimming Stadium had closed and that year's competition had been held in the Pontins holiday camp. It turned out that, while concrete was perfect for making grand architectural statements, longevity wasn't one of its qualities. Cracks in the structure had appeared the previous year and while councillors debated its future with some passion, it was decided that the economics didn't add up. The Super Swimming Stadium was omitted from that year's holiday brochure. Within the year, the 150,000 cubic yards of concrete had been removed and another slice of seaside heritage passed into history.

SCARBO

ROUGH

There's a sign on the outside of the Futurist building in Scarborough. It's formed from the same red plastic lettering once used to advertise the variety shows and latest films. Some of them are chipped, the colour faded a little, but the message is clear. It reads simply: 'That's All Folks'. The words have been up there since 6 January 2014, when the venue closed its doors for what many believe will be the last time. While at the time of writing a community group was putting together a business case for the place, any reprieve for the seafront theatre and cinema is likely only to be temporary. The land it stands on was identified as far back as 2010 as a 'fantastic opportunity site'. Those three little words, along with the fact the council can no longer afford to subsidise its running costs, may end up counting for more than the ninety-three-year history of a venue where The Beatles, Shirley Bassey, Ken Dodd and Morecambe and Wise all played.

'It's just so incredibly sad to see it there all boarded up,' says Patricia David, who, as founder of the campaign group, Save Our Futurist, has been desperately trying to rescue the venue from the bulldozers. 'It might not be as grand as some of the buildings in Scarborough, but it's an important part of our history.'

Patricia is right. The Futurist was never in the same league as the Victorian architecture which earned Scarborough the title the Queen of Watering Places. In the last few years of its life, when there were just a handful of families rattling around the vast auditorium watching the latest, slightly fuzzy blockbuster on the big screen, it took a little vision to imagine this was the same place where the opening of an American bar, with its 30ft-long marble bar, black and white tiled floor and Majolica glass lampshades, was the height of 1920s sophistication.

Yet, despite its slightly shabby appearance – the 1960s redesign which obscured the original Italian marble has not worn well – the threat of losing it forever has ignited a renewed love of the building. Whatever new development takes its place, it almost certainly won't include a theatre, and if, as seems likely, the Futurist is razed to the ground it will be the final curtain for a venue which has provided more than a century of entertainment in the resort's South Bay.

'The Arcadia was home to the Fairy River ride and it sounds quite incredible. It weaved through various grottos of exotic flowers before ending in a haunted forest.'

Previous pages: Charabancs, like this one photographed in the 1920s, were often used by companies to take their staff on work's outings.

Left: Entertainer Will Catlin began performing on the beach at Scarborough, but moved into the Arcadia, which later became the Futurist Theatre.

Opposite: Pierrot troupes were popular entertainment at many seaside resorts, often setting up temporary stages on which to perform.

Tony Peers is widely known in the resort as Mr Entertainment and he is both a promoter and fierce protector of the town.

'Back in 1903, the Kiralphi Brothers opened the Arcadia at the end of the South Bay where large fish warehouses once stood,' he says. 'The Arcadia was home to the Fairy River ride and it sounds quite incredible. It weaved through various grottos of exotic flowers before ending in a haunted forest. That was really the start, and ever since this little corner of Scarborough has been the backdrop for entertainment. None more so than when Will Catlin arrived here.'

Catlin remains one of the key figures in British seaside history. The Leicester-born entertainer came to perform in Scarborough as one half of a double act and liked the place so much he never left. Unlike many of those he shared a stage with,

Catlin was also blessed with a business brain and soon began organising his own troupes of Pierrots. Initially performing on the beach, he soon realised the advantage of having a permanent venue, one where rain and wind couldn't drive customers away, and moved into the Arcadia site. From his first all-male ensemble, featuring four or five performers, the troupe grew to a twenty-strong outfit. Each member, wearing immaculate evening dress, was not only required to sing and dance, but encouraged to project the image of a suave, eligible bachelor whether they were single or not. It was a winning combination and the stalls were often packed with women hoping to take home more than just a souvenir programme. Right up until his death in 1953 at the age of eighty-two, Catlin was still actively managing shows in Scarborough, as well as Llandudno and Great Yarmouth. At his funeral,

This page: Scarborough's popularity as a resort began in the seventeenth century with the discovery of spring waters.

a pointed Pierrot hat, made from white flowers, sat on top of his coffin. It was a fitting tribute to a man who had given much of his life to entertaining others.

By then, the Futurist, which had replaced the old Arcadia, was entering its own heyday. When it had opened in 1921, the theatre-cum-cinema, with its illuminated dome casting stars across the ceiling, seemed to borrow a little of the glamour of Hollywood.

Sadly, the Futurist won't be the first Scarborough landmark to become a victim of economics.

It was the discovery of spring waters by Thomasin Farrer around 1626 which transformed the fortunes of the town. Previously a down-on-its-luck coastal outpost, the erection of the first spa buildings at the turn of the eighteenth century by Dicky Dickinson, a man who reputedly made up for what he lacked in charm with entrepreneurial spirit, marked the start of the boom years. By the time that original complex ended up beneath a giant landslide in 1737, Scarborough had established itself at the forefront of medicinal bathing and hydrotherapy, attracting the wealthy seeking relaxation and entrepreneurs hoping to cash in on the influx of the fabulously rich.

'The Victorians were very ambitious, especially after the arrival of the railways,' explains local historian Trevor Pearson. 'However, some of those early money-making schemes were quite ill-thought-through.'

He points to the castle high up on the South Bay. Today, the cliffside is clad in a metal mesh to prevent rockfalls and there are not many who can walk to the top from the seafront without stopping to catch their breath at least once. Yet it was on this almost vertical drop that in the 1860s a man called Fairbank decided to open an ornamental rock garden.

'As part of the plans he also constructed a wooden arena to seat 3,000 people, or at least it would have done had anyone been able to get to it,' says Trevor. 'It might have looked impressive, but the path to it was so steep that only a handful of people ever managed to negotiate their way down. After just two years, Fairbank had to admit defeat and the gardens

were closed for good. The Victorian age was one where everything seemed possible, but often the end result fell some way short of the original grand designs.'

The same problem afflicted another ambitious scheme. At the same time as a small army of labourers was building Scarborough's cliffside railways, representatives from the Revolving Towers Company also arrived at the resort. The very first of these towers had been built in Atlantic City, New Jersey, and London engineer Thomas Warwick reckoned they would work just as well over here. It wasn't a bad idea. A wave of attractions was about to be imported from America and revolving towers no doubt seemed a more appealing prospect than the early glaciarium rinks made of hogs' lard instead of ice.

In Scarborough, the latticework structure's steam-powered platform slowly began to turn on the North Cliff in 1898, taking the first 200 people the 150ft to the top of the tower. It proved popular that summer, but behind the scenes the Revolving Towers Company was creaking. It had become clear that the revenue generated from ticket sales was falling far short of early estimates. Directors blamed Warwick, accusing him of mismanagement. Warwick blamed the directors for failing to make the towers sufficiently attractive and by 1900 a winding-up order had been issued. The Scarborough tower continued to operate for another seven years, but by the end of the first decade of the twentieth century it was no more.

Thankfully, the health-giving properties of the resort's waters proved more resilient. Two hundred and fifty years after the opening of the first spa, Scarborough remained a leading centre for hydrotherapy and Londesborough Lodge was its hub. Standing high on the South Bay with impressive sea views, the property had originally been the seaside residence of Baron Londesborough, who had bought the house set in a 6,000-acre estate in 1849. Later acquired by the Scarborough Corporation, in 1929 it reopened as an exclusive Turkish, Russian and electro-medical bathhouse.

Chauffeur-driven Rolls-Royces would pull up outside, the women dripping in furs and clutching large handbags and very small dogs. The Lodge was a magnet for the landed gentry and the elite of show business and sport. Others said less kindly that its clientele was made up of lush lords and ladies, choleric colonels and mad mayors, who often arrived straight from a shooting party or after having run up heavy losses at a gaming table.

It was often said that the calendar and the clock stopped at the Lodge as its guests spent hours being attended to by one of the dedicated masseuses or soaking in baths infused with seaweed gathered from the shore. Others came simply to relax in one of the lounges where the chairs were upholstered in tapestry, the carpets were of the very thickest pile and the conversation was always muted. To step into the Lodge was to step into a time capsule where an atmosphere of quiet contentment was prized above all else. Nothing ever changed, not even the staff.

However, in the early 1970s the outside world did catch up with one of the last bastions of Scarborough's great heritage. In 1967, 7,676 guests had attended the baths. Five years later, visitor numbers had dropped to just 2,217 and the Lodge was showing losses of £12,000 a year. Its refusal to move with the times had initially been its selling point, but ultimately it became its downfall. A number of other hotels had opened new spas and compared with those modern saunas the facilities at the Lodge, then one of the last remaining medicinal baths in the country, belonged to an earlier time. In December 1973, its closure was announced.

After a brief reincarnation as a museum of local history, the building has struggled to find a use in twenty-first century Scarborough. Put up for sale in 2009, the Buddhist Ropka Trust later expressed an interest in taking over the Grade II listed property and hope to turn it into a health and well-being clinic.

Back in 1973, as the Lodge's eight remaining staff began looking for other work, one of their regular clients, Jack Anderson, summed up the prevailing mood. The Scot, who had lived in Scarborough for thirty years, told the *Yorkshire Evening Post*: 'Today's resorts must fight for business, but I feel that in a place like this there must always be room for some sort of oasis and that is what the Lodge is to us. Just to sit here with a pot of coffee is relaxation. It would

Standing high on the South Bay with impressive sea views, the property had originally been the seaside residence of Baron Londesborough, who had bought the house set in a 6,000-acre estate in 1849. Later acquired by the Scarborough Corporation, in 1929 it reopened as an exclusive Turkish, Russian and electro-medical bathhouse.

make a wonderful private club and I would surely think that there is some method of preserving it for the public in a form that is not too different from the present one. After all we have little enough of our past left to treasure.'

It's a sentiment those currently battling to save the Futurist share. The campaign has adopted the tagline 'life without industry is guilt; industry without art is brutality' and has found support from some unlikely quarters, including from beyond the grave.

Recently they came across a stone slab at the rear of the building. Not only is it believed to be the last resting place of Will Catlin's younger brother, Tom, but campaigners claim the small plot is protected by a covenant put in place in 1961 preventing it from being disturbed without the permission of Catlin's Scarborough Entertainments Ltd. The company was wound up in 1989 and according to the council, which wants the site to be developed by nearby theme park Flamingo Land, that makes the covenant null and void. Can the ghost of seaside past save the Futurist? In Scarborough, stranger things have happened.

Opposite: Described as the Queen of Watering Places, Scarborough with its grand Victorian architecture was the premier resort on the East Coast.

SCARBOROUGH NORTH YORKSHIRE 175

CLEETH

ORPES

On the evening of 20 December 1976, Cleethorpes' Winter Gardens earned a place in the history of punk rock.

There was always an air of unpredictability about Sex Pistols gigs, but that night the atmosphere was even more heightened. Just a couple of weeks earlier, Johnny Rotten and Sid Vicious had found themselves at the centre of a media storm having created some of the most memorable few minutes in British television history. The band's now infamous appearance on *Today* with Bill Grundy was always going to be risky. Broadcast live, just after teatime, it started badly and got worse. These were the days when Mary Whitehouse and the National Viewers' and Listeners' Association had already branded a seemingly innocent episode of *Dr Who* 'teatime brutality for tots' and by the time the credits rolled telephone lines were jammed with callers complaining about the bad language.

Thames Television issued a hurried apology and Grundy, whose career would never recover from the incident, was initially suspended for two weeks. In the days that followed, EMI chairman John Read announced the company was reconsidering its two-year contract with the band worth £40,000 and venues already booked for the Sex Pistols' Anarchy

in the UK tour began to pull out. Of the nineteen planned dates, just three went ahead, including the one at the Winter Gardens a few days before Christmas.

Manager Jimmy Jackson later claimed he had been unaware of the furore, but a few sweary teenagers were hardly a match for the former RAF man who always wore a tuxedo to every gig.

'I knew it was going to be a lively do and by God it was,' said Jimmy on the thirtieth anniversary of the concert. 'They whipped their audience up into frenzy, which was something we had to watch out for. It was a great relief when it was all over.'

In the end, the anarchic spirit of 1976 resulted in just a few scuffles and three broken windows. Nevertheless, the presence of the Sex Pistols could hardly have been more different from the tea dances that had packed out the ballroom in the early days of the Winter Gardens. While many seaside resorts owed their grand architecture to wealthy businessmen, Cleethorpes' iconic building was the result of an unfortunate accident involving Lincolnshire railway worker George Eyre.

Details of the incident are scant, but having received a generous compensation package after both his legs were amputated, George decided

Previous pages: An early colour postcard shows families on the beach at Cleethorpes in the summer of 1910.

Opposite: In the nineteenth century Cleethorpes was a small fishing village, but a century on it had developed into a major seaside resort.

Above: Having cost £8,000 to build, the 1,200ft pier at Cleethorpes was officially opened on the August bank holiday of 1873.

that he would secure his future by building an 'amusement hall and restaurant'. His wife, Rose, already owned a plot of land and, with the planning application approved, work began in 1934.

Known originally as the Olympia, it might not have been as smartly designed as the Winter Gardens at Blackpool and Morecambe, but it gave Cleethorpes a venue where holidaymakers could head should the weather turn, something even a resort which would later boast its own weather prophet needed.

Harry Brown was a nightwatchman at a pumping station in the 1950s, a job which offered ample opportunity to study cloud formations and predict the following day's weather. So detailed and reliable were his forecasts that they were sent to railway stations in Leeds, Doncaster and Barnsley in the hope of encouraging people to the coast, and when Harry promised sunshine those who ran the town's attractions said they noticed a definite increase in holiday traffic. He was clearly talented, but even Harry couldn't prevent a bank holiday downpour.

Whatever the weather, however, the Winter Gardens was always open for business.

It changed its name following the Second World War when it had been used as a cookhouse and dining area for the 8th Reserve Royal Artillery. By then the building was no longer owned by the Eyres. George had been forced to sell up following the death of his wife. Rose, it turned out, had not made a will and with various family members demanding a slice of the value of her land, the building was put on the market and the money used to appease warring relations.

Now it was the turn of local baker Don Twidale to usher in a new era at the Winter Gardens.

It was he who set up the Saturday night dances, but it was under Jimmy Jackson's reign in the 1960s that it became the region's premier music venue. It was Jimmy who asked Jack Lawton and Shirley King to run a variety night at the Gardens. Jack was the organist on the pier and having married Shirley, who was regularly described as the East Coast's answer to Dame Vera Lynn, the couple were a formidable double act. As well as the Saturday Night Continental show, an unashamed wallow in nostalgia, there were

the Friday afternoon tea dances, and so wedded to the venue was Shirley that even after she stopped performing, she continued as its marketing and promotions officer until her retirement in 1990.

During the Lawton and King heyday, the Winter Gardens thrived. Its aim was to cater for everyone and it also inspired one young teenage boy to devote his life to the music business. Stephen Stanley was just fourteen when he walked into the venue for his very first concert in 1970.

'One of the really special things about the Winter Gardens was it had an all-age licence. I'll always remember that Sunday. The rock band playing was called Mezziah and the lead singer happened to be the brother of one of my school friends. I was there pretty much every Sunday after that. It was mostly progressive rock bands and the same acts came round again and again, but you know what the funny thing was? We'd all sit on the floor and the listen to the music, there was no big crush at the front, no mosh pit. I think we were modelling ourselves on footage we'd seen from that first ever Glastonbury.'

Known originally as the Olympia, it might not have been as smartly designed as the Winter Gardens at Blackpool and Morecambe, but it gave Cleethorpes a venue where holidaymakers could head should the weather turn, something even a resort which would later boast its own weather prophet needed.

While the facilities inside the Winter Gardens were fairly basic and the structure unlikely to have passed today's rigorous health and safety checks, it was the social hub of Cleethorpes, providing both a platform for upcoming bands and a backdrop for countless civic dinners.

'It attracted some really big names,' says Stephen. 'When Queen played it was packed to capacity and the queue still stretched round the block. It's incredible to think now, but AC/DC played there, so did Steve Harley & Cockney Rebel and Roxy Music. The Winter Gardens was the perfect size for bands on their way up and those on their way back down.'

As for many of Cleethorpes' teenagers, the Winter Gardens became Stephen's second home. So when towards the late 1970s the live acts began to dry up, he decided to give music promotion a go himself.

'Nearly a year went by without there being a Thursday night gig. I asked the management why they had stopped booking acts and they just said that it wasn't financially viable. I wasn't buying that, so I asked how much it was to hire the venue for the night. They told me it would be £60. Now that was a lot of money back then, but I had the naivety of youth on my side. I was going to put on a concert.'

With a blank contacts book, Stephen decided to chance his arm by going direct to some of the country's biggest record labels in the hope of securing a big name for the bill.

Opposite: The Olympia, the forerunner to the Winter Gardens, was built by railway worker George Eyre using compensation money from an industrial accident.

Right: The resort expanded quickly in the late nineteenth century when the railway connected Cleethorpes with the industrial towns and cities of Yorkshire.

'It seems funny now, but I honestly rang EMI to see if they had anyone who would like to play the Winter Gardens. They didn't take much notice of my request, so I thought, "Right, I'm just going to start at the top by writing to Paul McCartney". Needless to say, I didn't get a response.'

With time ticking on, Stephen approached Rough Trade Records, an independent label with a number of upcoming acts on their books. A few phone calls and a little haggling later, an eclectic sounding trio featuring Prag-Veg, Monochrome Set and Manicured Noise were signed up for the inaugural concert on 25 July 1979.

'It was a brilliant night, but I remember the next day working out the finances. I'd paid £300 for the bands and with the cost of advertising, printing the tickets I worked out that I had lost 72p. That should have told me something about the promotion business.'

It didn't. Solid Entertainments was born. Stephen was responsible for bringing a succession of bands to the Winter Gardens throughout the 1980s, all performing under the watchful eye of Jimmy Jackson.

'Jimmy was the Winter Gardens. He always wore a tuxedo, even when the place had become a little run-down. I remember the night The Pogues played. They came in at 5p.m. to do the soundcheck and at that point were completely sober. After they finished,

Above: By the time this photograph was taken in 1978, traditional ballroom dances had long given way to something altogether more modern.

Left: Before a performance at the Winter Gardens, country music singer Frank Ifield had time for cup of tea with the venue's proprietor Jimmy Jackson.

Opposite: In the 1950s, the resort was popular with families from across Yorkshire and Lincolnshire.

Jimmy turned to me and said, "Well, they seem like a nice folk group, this is the kind of band we should be booking". Of course, by the time they actually got on stage a few hours later they had drunk four slabs of lager in their dressing room and a lot more besides. It was mayhem, but even on the most chaotic of nights, you couldn't ruffle Jimmy. You might have been able to see a slight look of horror written on his face, but he never said a word.'

From the top of the building it was possible to see across the River Humber and all the way to Spurn Point. In later years, it also offered a bird's-eye view of the holidaymakers queuing for the ferry to take them to Zeebrugge, a gateway to the rest of Europe. That snaking line was not good news for Cleethorpes, but for a while at least the Winter Gardens seemed immune from the changing fortunes of Britain's seaside resorts.

Above: After the Sex Pistols' appearance on Today with Bill Grundy there were only a handful of dates left on the 1976 Anarchy in the UK tour as many venues pulled out. However, Cleethorpes' Winter Gardens was one of the few that welcomed Johnny Rotten and Sid Vicious.

Opposite: The venue might not have been architecturally beautiful, but it provided a focal point for the resort's entertainment offering.

'They whipped their audience up into frenzy, which was something we had to watch out for. It was a great relief when it was all over.'

Along with the Wigan Casino and Manchester's Twisted Wheel, the venue had become known for holding one of the country's biggest and best Northern Soul nights. Hundreds would descend on the Winter Gardens to dance to the likes of Frank Wilson's 'Do I Love You (Indeed I Do)' and 'You Didn't Say a Word' by Yvonne Baker, and when the last record was played those who didn't have jobs to go to would head down to the seafront to end the night with an early morning serving of fish and chips. Most nights of the week the Winter Gardens remained busy, not least on Wednesdays when the Bags Ball – so-called because of the high number of female divorcees prowling the dance floor – opened for business.

The venue survived the recession of the early 1990s, it survived the exodus of holidaymakers to foreign shores, but the Winter Gardens wasn't invincible. In 2007, it was announced that the building had been sold to developers. Even when it was boarded up, those who had grown up on its dance floor still hoped there might be a last-minute reprieve. There wasn't. Following a spate of vandalism, the decision was taken to clear the site. In its place was supposed to be a new housing development, but, as the demolition began, the economy nose-dived. The development money dried up and the land was turned into a car park.

'It should have been preserved,' says Stephen. 'If I'd have won the lottery I would have bought it myself. The community of Cleethorpes was lost the day they bulldozed the Winter Gardens. It was more than just a place where bands played and as soon as it went you could feel the whole town quietly start to deteriorate.'

However, the rot seems to have stopped. In 2013, Cleethorpes house prices rocketed. The town enjoyed the biggest leap in coastal property prices in the last ten years and it seems likely that the old car park will be turned over to housing. Elsewhere there are plans for a sympathetic restoration of the 140-year-old pier and, while many might have scoffed at the suggestion a decade ago, there is a belief in Cleethorpes that it can reinvent itself as the Southwold of the North. The only thing it won't have, though, is a Winter Gardens.

B   A   N

G O R

Shortly after 5 p.m. on 14 August 1969, 300 troops from the 1st Battalion, Prince of Wales's Own Regiment of Yorkshire marched into the centre of Derry following three days and two nights of rioting. The annual Protestant Apprentice Boys' parade through the largely Catholic Bogside area of the city had provided the flashpoint, but despite tensions mounting in the Province, the British government insisted its soldiers would be gone in a couple of days once order had been restored.

That same Friday night, seventy miles away at the coast, life was continuing as normal in Bangor. A fleet of fishing boats bobbed in the harbour as the hotels, restaurants and guesthouses prepared for another busy weekend in the summer season. Even when reports of events in Derry appeared in the next day's newspapers, few worried too much about the consequences.

However, within a few months the ripple effect of the violence had hit the coast. The troops hadn't left; in fact, they would be a permanent presence on the streets for decades to come and repeated television footage showing petrol bombings, barricades and riot shields being employed did little for Northern Ireland's image abroad. The following year, several large travel companies reported that bookings were 50 per cent down on those in 1968. All agreed that the falling-off was 'due to the Troubles or rumour of Troubles' and, paradoxically, the areas where no violence had been witnessed seemed the worst affected.

As one Bangor guesthouse owner at the time said: 'None of our visitors saw as much as a broken window last year and I am sure they will not this year. Two English women who have been coming to us for years came again recently and told me they had been doing their best to persuade their friends that there was no reason why anyone should not come here for a holiday. They had to admit that they could not convince them that terrible things were not happening all the time all over Northern Ireland.'

A major advertising campaign was being planned to mark the fiftieth anniversary of the signing of Northern Ireland's constitution and its decision to opt out of the Irish Free State, but it did little good. The only hotels which could count business as brisk were the Conway and Royal Avenue in Belfast, the unofficial headquarters for the world's press. Tourism was on hold and towns like Bangor would never be the same again.

'I'm sure we all look back at our childhood as a fairly idyllic time where the sun always shone,' says lifelong Bangor resident Brian Wilson. 'It might not be quite true, but before everything changed Bangor was a pretty perfect place to grow up. You had the beach on your doorstep, the countryside was ten minutes away and there was that buzz that only seaside resorts have. The idea that hundreds of people would get on a ferry from Scotland to come to where you live was really exciting. We'd just come through the austerity of the 1950s, and the 1960s did feel like a period of social revolution. The tourists brought Bangor to life, but the decade which began with such a great amount of idealism ended with frustration and a sign of the years of violence to come.

'The whole atmosphere of the place changed in the 1970s. We're just ten miles from Belfast and while we were fairly isolated from the Troubles themselves there was a big exodus from the capital to places like Bangor. By the time the Good Friday Agreement was signed in 1998, Bangor had become a commuter town.'

By then, along with countless hotels and guesthouses, it had also seen three of its most memorable structures consigned to history. While the resort had its roots in the Victorian age when it was marketed as 'Northern Ireland's answer to Brighton', it was the architects of the 1930s who stamped a brand new style on the resort with the building of Pickie Pool, Caproni's dance hall and, most iconic of them all, the Tonic cinema. Commissioned by Bangor businessman John O'Neill, who funded the project through the sale of his fleet

Previous pages: Bangor may be a much quieter resort today than it was in the 1960s, but a string of golf clubs and a marina continue to attract tourists.

Opposite: The town was popular with holidaymakers from the late nineteenth century, but Bangor really came into its own during the 1930s.

MAIN St. BANGOR Co. DOWN. 4734 W.L.

of Tonic buses, the Art Deco design was down to the architect, John McBride Neill. In just two years he had been responsible for six other cinemas in Ireland, but the Tonic was to be his crowning glory. Built in seven months for £76,000, when it was completed in 1936, with its illuminated glass tower, shops and flats, it was the second largest cinema in the whole of Ireland. However, even its 2,250 seats weren't enough to accommodate the crowd waiting to see Ronald Colman in *The Man Who Broke the Bank at Monte Carlo* on opening night. Grabbing a megaphone to address the queue outside, the manager made a deal. While the auditorium was already full, he said they could come in as long as they were happy to sit in the aisles.

'It was incredibly luxurious with thick carpets and the lift seemed incredibly modern at the time,' says Helen McCormick, who grew up in Bangor just a few streets from the Tonic. 'There was a large stage in front of the screen with multiple curtains which could be closed for live performances and below was the magnificent

Compton organ, which would rise up to be played during the intervals. The sound was just incredible.

'During the war the place was always packed as Bangor was full of soldiers waiting to be stationed abroad. Regiments from England, Scotland and Wales were based here and the queue stretched around the building most evenings.'

It was a similar story at Caproni's dance hall. Run by an Italian family, the venue might not have been quite as lavish as the cinema, but it had by all accounts the best sprung dance floor in Bangor.

'We didn't realise at the time, but it was all quite formal,' says Brian, a regular at Caproni's during the 1960s. 'Without fail, Mr Caproni would be on the door checking that everyone was abiding by the dress code. I remember one night he turned a group of girls away for wearing trouser suits. He didn't approve; he thought girls should wear skirts or dresses.

'The other thing, of course, was there was no alcohol on sale. People came for the music and to dance and the bands were under strict instruction

Bangor had pretty much everything a seaside resort needed and the opening of Pickie Pool in 1937 gave it another popular meeting spot. As with most open-air pools in Britain, the water was never particularly warm. In fact, it was generally freezing, but taking a dip was a rite of passage for the youngsters, wrapped in towels sneaked out of guesthouses, who shivered on the tiered concrete and wooden benches.

that they had to finish at midnight on the dot. Anyone who overran, even by a couple of minutes, would have the plug pulled. You were never in doubt who was in charge at Caproni's.'

Bangor had pretty much everything a seaside resort needed and the opening of Pickie Pool in 1937 gave it another popular meeting spot. As with most open-air pools in Britain, the water was never particularly warm. In fact, it was generally freezing, but taking a dip was a rite of passage for the youngsters, wrapped in towels sneaked out of guesthouses, who shivered on the tiered concrete and wooden benches.

While the Troubles effectively suspended tourism in Northern Ireland, they weren't solely to blame for Bangor's decline as a seaside resort or the loss of three of its best-loved attractions.

Caproni's lost out as rival venues, selling alcohol, began to open; indoor leisure centres with their heated pools and spacious changing rooms proved more enticing than a windswept concrete lido; and with the expansion of the television schedules – BBC2, launched in 1964, and ITV, with its emphasis on light entertainment, was pulling in higher and higher ratings – a trip to the cinema was no longer the event it had been a decade or so earlier.

The last dance took place at Caproni's on 14 July 1983, and by the end of the decade Pickie Pool had been filled in to make way for a new marina development. The decline of the cinema was more gradual, but no less painful to watch.

In 1969, the Tonic's famous organ was bought by Rodney Bambrick for just £150, who had it installed at Bangor's new boys' school where he was head of history, but while the old cinema struggled on, there were some days when there were more staff than customers. The Tonic cinema's size had once been

its claim to fame, but fashions changed and now on most Saturday afternoons the large auditorium, already gutted of its 1930s glamour, looked a little sad. By the early 1980s, John McBride Neill's masterpiece stood as a symbol of faded grandeur and Belfast Cinemas Ltd announced its closure. The last ever film to be screened there was *WarGames* in 1983. It was a film about the Cold War, about technology and the rise of computers. Since the Tonic had first opened its doors in 1936, the world had moved on and those plush carpets and opulent lighting now looked strangely old-fashioned.

'No one knew quite what to do with the place, but the cinema had been listed, so we thought it would be at least protected until another use could be found,' says Brian, who has been a local councillor in Bangor for more than thirty years. 'Part of the problem was that it was just so big and there just wasn't the interest from developers. Stood empty, it became a bit of an eyesore. It was a target for vandals and a cover for drug-taking. Understandably, those who lived nearby wanted something done.'

Finally, in the winter of 1991, the council proposed that the Tonic should be converted into sheltered housing and unveiled plans showing the ground floor given over to shops and smart first-floor apartments. They were never realised. Six months later, before work had begun, a fire ripped through the building. A few days later it was demolished.

'That was a sad day for Bangor,' says Brian. 'The Tonic was such a landmark and suddenly it was gone.'

Residential homes were built on the site of both the Tonic and Caproni's, a sign perhaps of Bangor's shifting demographic. The only thing that remains of either is the organ, but that, too, now lies in storage, dismantled. The old school building in which it had happily sat for almost forty years was itself

Above: There may not have been buckets and spades, but the sands of Bangor were always a draw for the young, with this part dubbed Children's Corner.

demolished in 2008. Rodney, then long retired, tried desperately to find a new home for his beloved instrument, now the only one of its kind in Northern Ireland, and for a while it looked like it might be taken by Bangor Grammar School. However, the cost of installation was high and the trust set up to preserve the organ for future generations has so far struggled to find funding.

'Bangor has had to find a new direction,' says Brian. 'As much as we'd have all loved to see it return to the bustling seaside resort it was before the 1970s, that was never going to happen. The tourists we get now tend to come for the half a dozen golf clubs near here and the marina which opened towards the end of the 1980s has been good for the place. You can't keep looking back, but I do feel lucky to have been born when I was. I think I got to see Bangor at its very best.'

BIBLIOGRAPHY

Anon, *Seaside Watering Places*, 1897–8.

Armstrong, Keith, *The Spanish City: The Heart and Soul of Whitley Bay in Words and Pictures*, Northern Voices Community Project, 2010.

Copnall, Stephen, *Pleasureland Memories*, Skelter Publishing, 2005.

Endacott, Sylvia and Shirley Lewis, *Butlin's 75 Years of Fun*, The History Press, 2011.

Gray, Fred, *Walking on Water: The West Pier Story*, Brighton West Pier Trust, 1998.

Green, John W. and Robin A. Money, *Exploring the History of Lee-on-the-Solent*, Chaplin Books, 2013.

Hardy, Dennis and Colin Ward, *Arcadia for All: The Legacy of a Makeshift Landscape*, Five Leaves Publications, 2003.

Lyons, Mary, *The Story of the Jaywick Sands Estate*, Phillimore, 1996.

Markham, John, *Rose Carr*, The North Holderness Museum of Village Life, 1981.

Pearson, Lynn F, *Piers and other Seaside Architecture*, Shire Library, 2002.

Pertwee, Bill, *Beside the Seaside*, Collins & Brown, 1999.

Pitcairn-Knowles, Richard, *Celebrating the Centenary of the Founding of Riposo Health Hydro in Hastings 1912–2012*, 2012.

Rotherham, Ian D., *Spas and Spa Visiting*, Shire Publications, 2014.

Sharp, Mick, *The Dome of Memories*, Black Dog Design, 2011.

PICTURE CREDITS